LANDMARK COLLECTOR'S LIBRARY

The Spirit of
LEEK:3
THE TEXTILE MILLS

Cathryn Walton & Lindsey Porter

Lindsey Porter　　　*Cathryn Walton*

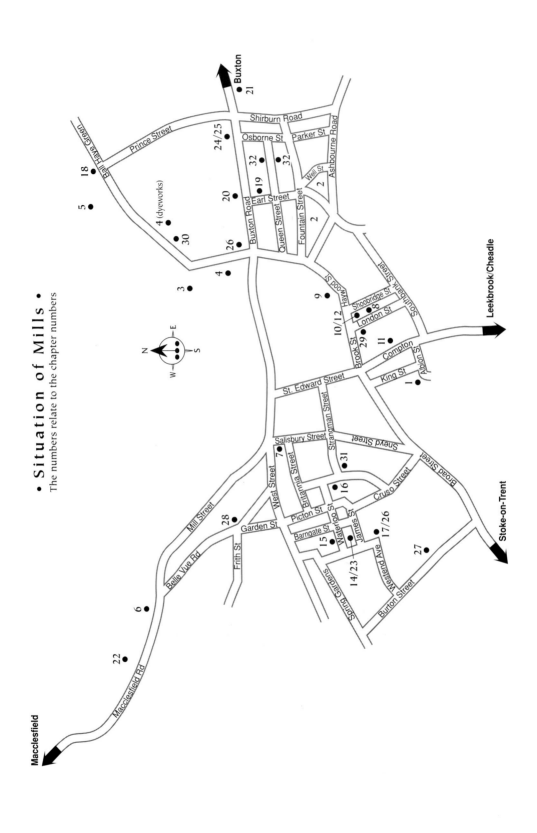

• Situation of Mills •
The numbers relate to the chapter numbers

LANDMARK COLLECTOR'S LIBRARY

THE SPIRIT OF
LEEK:3
• THE TEXTILE MILLS •

Cathryn Walton & Lindsey Porter

Landmark Publishing

Published by

Ashbourne Hall, Cokayne Ave
Ashbourne, Derbyshire DE6 1EJ England
Tel: (01335) 347349 Fax: (01335) 347303
e-mail: landmark@clara.net
web site: www.landmarkpublishing.co.uk

1st edition

ISBN 1 84306 031 0

Printed by Bookcraft, Bath

Design & reproduction by James Allsopp

Cover captions:

Front cover: New machinery for Hope Silk Mills, 1959
Back cover top: Half Hose Knitting Dept, Job White & Sons
Back cover middle: Wardle & Davenport's former mill
Back cover bottom: Dyehouse men at Joshua Wardles

Page 1: The machine room for dresses, Moorland Mill, Job Whites
Page 3: Dressing machines, Leek Spun Silk,1915

CONTENTS

Brough Nicholson & Hall

ACKNOWLEDGEMENTS

Acordis UK Ltd; Aerofilms; Ann Arnold; Valerie Bagnall; Dorothy Bloor; John Bould; Ken Bowyer; Catherine Braddock and the staff of Leek Library; Mr & Mrs E Bratt; Linda Brown; Donald Campion; Mrs Charnock; Mrs Barbara Clay; Mr & Mrs A Clews; Mrs J Day; Mrs S Done; Ralph & Irene Fleming; Yvonne & Lynton Goldstraw; Graham Grindey; Marian Hulme; Jane Jones; Susan Keates and late George Keates; Leek and District Historical Society; Leek and Moorlands Historical Trust; Leek Town Council; Ray Lovatt; Carol Lowndes; Gerald Mee; Noel Moorhouse; John & Margaret Oliver; Mr & Mrs George Oultram; Muriel Pakeman; Ray Poole; Debbie Potts; Mr & Mrs Stan Prime; David Rhead; Ann Sharratt; Vin Smith; Staffordshire Record Office; Miss P Starling; Basil & Kathleen Turner; Mrs Watson; Pam Webb; Maureen Whiston; E H Whittles; Kathleen Wilson

Opportunities? They're limitless in the Textile Industry

INTRODUCTION

Having produced two books prior to this, it was clear that we had enough material for a volume devoted to the textile mills and the town's dyeworks. Even now, having completed the compilation of this book, we have some large omissions. We have also excluded works beyond the town, with the exception of Joshua Wardle at Leekbrook. Consequently, the Tatton's dyeworks at Upperhulme; their works at Mayfield and elsewhere; plus Brough's mill at Cheadle do not feature here. The selection of photographs used varies enormously, from social events to the more detailed photographs of many of the departments at Job White.

We are conscious that what we have portrayed is nothing more than a fleeting glance in what were often essential elements of the lives of many people down the generations. Textiles and dyeing were such a fundamental part of the livelihood of the town that it's difficult to appreciate that it has all changed. How odd it now appears to read the *Leek Post & Times* headline (above) which led a careers feature of the industry in the 1960s.

Our selection of images also mainly excludes the steam engines which drove the factories; many of the products produced by the companies featured and ancillary industries such as Buxton's box works on Buxton Road. Nonetheless, what we have portrayed hopefully gives a good insight into Leek's textile industry as a whole. We hope it brings back many memories and serves as a lasting reminder of the former industry of the town.

We have deliberated over how we arranged the order of the companies. We hope the arrangment chosen is the most convenient. Finally, this book is an endeavour to bring together a reminder of an industry in which neither of the author's have worked, other than for a short period of time. We have therefore relied extensively on peoples' memories.

ALBION MILL

Anthony Ward established a sewing thread manufactury here in the early years of the 19th century. At least ten power looms operated in this silk mill in 1839.

Albion Mill was gradually extended over the years, a new section was completed in 1924 and an additional 'copping' room established in 1955. Cops were cardboard tubes which had thread wound onto them. A new packing room was built in 1963. 150 years of business was celebrated by Wards on 18th May, 1963. The festivities took place at the Southbank Hotel which, incidentally, was the former home of the Ward family.

In later years the firm's main markets were in manufacturing sewing threads used in footwear, upholstery, lifting slings, safety harnesses, flexible containers and lingerie.

Morgan's animal food plant occupied a part of Albion Mill in the 1990s and at one time a room was used for the manufacture of football strips. Albion Mill, a listed building, with its decorative bell tower, now stands empty. Proposals have been made to convert the mill to flats in the same way that Brunswick and Wellington Mills have been converted

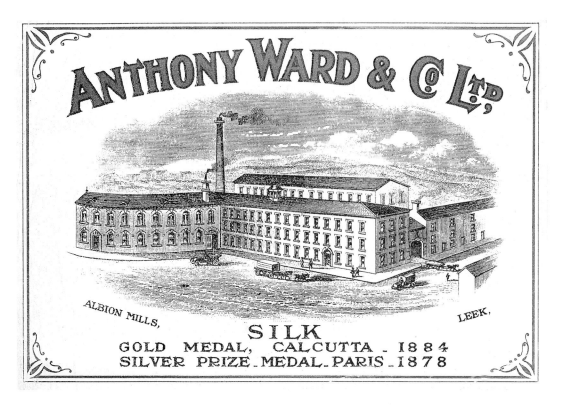

Above: An artist's impression of Albion Mill and the houses in King Street. When the mill was built it faced open countryside

Below: A 'reps' calling card with illustrations of Anthony Ward's sewing thread logos

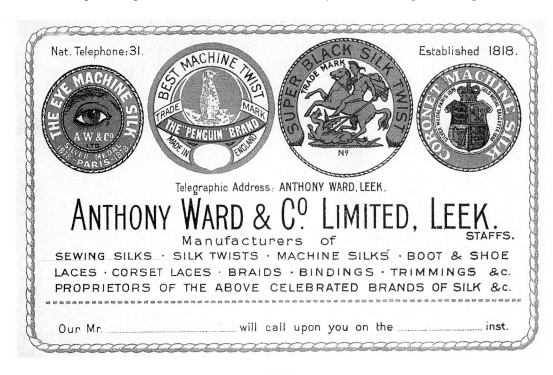

Left: John Ward 1878-1955, eldest son of Anthony Ward junior, is pictured here by garages which opened into Albion Street. In earlier years these garages were part of stables and a coach house – Mrs Anthony Ward could often be seen, in the 1920s, riding in a black landeau drawn by two black horses

Below left: Major Bertram Townsend Ward. The second son of Anthony Ward junior, he attended Rossall School. While studying there he held the record for the Public School one mile championship which he ran in 4 minutes 33$\frac{1}{4}$ seconds at Stamford Bridge. Bertram Ward was a director of Anthony Ward together with his brother John

Below right: John Newall, Peter Proctor, Sam Bradshaw, Louis Bain, Ensor Barks and Harry Palk, all executives of Anthony Ward, pictured outside the front door of Albion Mill in 1974

This aerial view shows the former extent of this large works, stretching almost from The Monument to Portland Street. Note also, Myatts and Worthingtons in Queen Street, Premier Dyeworks and Tattons on Buxton Road, plus Whites, Clemesha's Dyeworks and CWS Ltd on, or just off, Ball Haye Road. Copyright: Aerofilms

Fountain Mill was situated on the corner of Fountain Street and Well Street. The police station now occupies this site. Broughs took over the mill from Messrs George H Bermingham & Co. In 1907 Broughs installed machinery in Fountain Mill for the production of spun silk

YORK MILL

This mill in Ashbourne Road was built in 1898. It was named York Mill to commemorate a visit to Leek by the Duke and Duchess of York in 1900

Below left: A crane towers above York Mill in April 2001 as the water tower is

demolished. Part of the water tower had fallen through the kitchen roof of a house in Well Street. During the Second World War the walkway around the top of the water tower was used for fire watching

Below right: A bird's eye view of Well Street where a giant crane moves machinery. The tall chimney is no longer with us, just the base still stands to remind us of the hive of industrial activity which hummed around these narrow streets. The building to the immediate left of the chimney still stands as does Alexandra Mill in the right background. Concrete Mill, in Fountain Street, with its north-light roof, has been demolished

CROSS STREET MILL

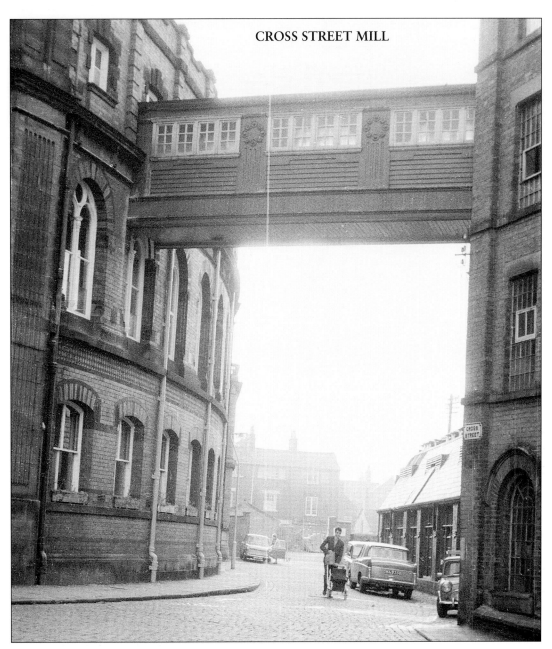

A view from Well Street looking into Cross Street. The end of Fountain Mill can be seen on the right. The buildings on the right have all been demolished, but Cross Street Mill on the left still stands. William Sugden designed the warehouse and offices in Cross Street in a classical style in the 1860s and his son Larner was responsible for the extension to the junction with Well Street, built in 1898.

The walkway which connected the two mills has long gone but its position can still be discovered by looking at the façade of the building on the left. A tunnel ran under the road which also linked the factories, so that the mills on Ashbourne Road, the warehouse on Cross Street and the mills in Fountain Street and Well Street could all be accessed without braving the elements. Some young women would rather have ventured outside than go along the underground tunnel as it was not unknown for a rat to be around!

Above: Looking towards Well Street from Cross Street, showing the bridge from the ware-house to Fountain Mill. The cobbles and the buildings are no more, but the area has been renovated in recent years with imitation gas lamps, black bollards lining the pavement and a road surface reflecting days of old

Below: In 1983, the Company's Cross Street Mill was taken over by Berresford's the ribbon manufacturers. Cross Street Mill has been saved for posterity, but the sign denoting the entrance pictured here has disappeared. Today's sign informs us that the mill now houses Moorlands Arts and Craft Centre, Anvil Antiques, Kiddies Kingdom and the Art Café

HOPE MILL

Back row: W Tatton, F Lovatt, H Finney, John Mien, W Billings, C Malkin. Middle row: Jeremiah Mien, J Turner, W Brady, J Clowes, J Bould (Foreman), N Tatton, G Clowes, W Bould. Front row: J Lomas, J Proctor, J Edge, F Lowndes, J O'Brien, T Smith.

These were the men of B N & H who successfully raised the roof of the Hope Mill to make another storey in the mill, without accident. The entire weight of the roof was about 280 tons. The roof was raised with lifting jacks, 3 inches at a time. This job was completed in about 10 weeks. The length of the room was 90 feet long and 30 feet wide. The roof was put back into position by the above joiners and bricklayers

Below left: A Morris 1000 van is parked on the cobbles of Fountain Street outside Hope Mill. Above Hope Mill is Concrete Mill, then the Fountain Inn and houses which were once rented to employees of Brough, Nicholson and Hall. On the extreme edge of the photograph is Fountain Mill. In 1966 Broughs specialised in braids, braided cords, lacing and crepe cords, braided ties, fancy trimmings, gymnasium girdles, wilting cords, boot, shoe and corset laces, embroidered badges, woven labels, ribbons, seam bindings, petershams, shoulder strappings, hat bands, blazer bindings and regalia ribbons!

Below right: Looking down Fountain Street with Concrete Mill beyond the Fountain Inn. The vast Brough, Nicholson and Hall site between Fountain Street and Cross Street was demolished in the late 1960s. The Health Centre, the Social Services building and the Police Station now stand on the site once occupied by the buildings depicted here. The Fountain Inn is the sole survivor

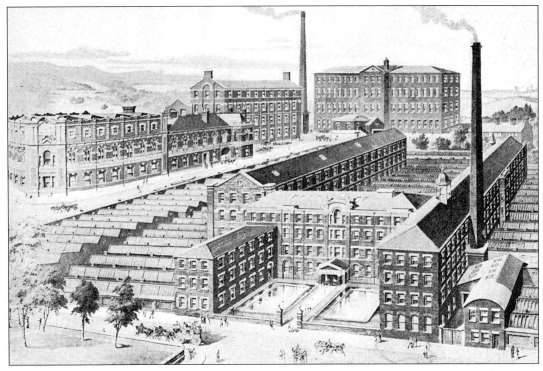

Above: The ponds in front of Hope Mill can be clearly seen in this stylised drawing. The Brough, Nicholson and Hall complex was able to treat the raw silk and process it until it reached the finished product. The mills had their own joinery, box and printing shops. During the wars, Broughs played a part in supplying the armed forces. They made miles of parachute cord, medal ribbons and webbing

Below: Hope Mill in Fountain Street was established by Thomas Carr in the 1820s. In 1851, when Mr Carr was manufacturing silk thread here, there was a fish pond, stocked with 600 goldfish, in front of Hope Mill. The pond was enclosed with palisades and supplied with fresh water from the engine pump. Many Leek people will remember Hope Mill when it was owned

by Brough Nicholson and Hall; it had two ponds in front of it even then. Hope Mill and the buildings on the west side of Cross Street were demolished in 1968. The Health Centre now occupies this site

July · 28th · 1900 ·

Opening · of · the
Leek Technical
Schools
By
HRH The Duchess of York

Laying · the
Foundation Stone
OF · THE
Gymnasium
BY
HRH The Duke of York

CHEADLE MILLS

LONDON WAREHOUSE 112 WOOD ST E.C.

LEEK WAREHOUSE

Brough Nicholson & Hall's
· MILLS · visited · by · THEIR ·
ROYAL HIGHNESSES
· on · the · same · day ·

This artist's impression shows the extent of the premises occupied by Brough, Nicholson and Hall, which stretched from Fountain Street through Well Street and Cross Street to the mills on Ashbourne Road. Brough, Nicholson and Hall were major employees in Leek having 1,000 employees by the 1920s. Their mills covered several acres and contained in excess of 70 rooms connected by rambling corridors. Young women who started to work at Broughs were often frightened of getting lost in the premises

These two photographs give us the names of the main departments. Eagle-eyed readers will notice that Fountain Mill is refered to as Canton Mill and was later increased in height by two stories

Fire at Broughs about the time of the Great War

Bridge End Dyeworks. The men here, in formal pose, are dyers working for Brough, Nicholson and Hall who owned the dyeworks before the Second World War. Later the works were acquired by Sir T & A Wardle's. Standing left to right:- W Tomlinson, W Gibson, Joe Bowcock, Jim Kirkland, Harold Tatton, ? Pickford, Jack Gayes jnr, Arthur Tomlinson, Charlie Rushton, Bill Brough, Frank Kelsall, George Aires, Bill Plant jnr, Charlie Gayes.
Sitting left to right:- ? Clewlow, Archie Rushton, Steve Yates, George Plant snr, Jim Bowcock, Will Earls, Harry Stonehewer, George H Rushton, Charlie James, George Hulme, Bill Plant.
Sitting on floor left to right:- Maurice Bowcock, Bill Cooper, Len Clay, Harold Jones, George Trafford

Far right: Prince Albert talking to Faulkner Nicholson as they leave Hope Mill during a visit on 1st July, 1931. Also pictured are Howe Hall, and B R Hall

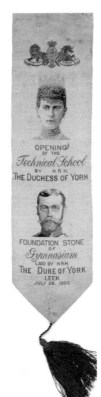

Below: Employees enjoyed many work's outings in the company's heyday

The

Coronation

of Their Majesties

King George VI.

and

Queen Elizabeth,

May 12th, 1937

VISIT of EMPLOYEES of

Brough, Nicholson & Hall Ltd., Leek,

to LONDON to see the CORONATION PROCESSION as guests of the Company.

BROUGH NICHOLSON & HALL LTD

1951

WORKS OUTING TO THE

FESTIVAL OF BRITAIN

Saturday June 23rd 1951

PROGRAMME

LEEK   STAFFS

Top: Girls winding silk

Middle: This page: Jacquard smallware looms for the production of petersham ribbons, grograms, silk hat bands, badges, labels and galons were introduced into Broughs in 1889. After an adjustment had been made beaded galloons could be produced. The beads came in packets of one hundred thousand ready threaded onto short strings which had to be transferred to continuous thread, wound onto small bobbins for weaving before producing designs sometimes further embellished with sequins

Bottom: Ladies sitting in front of the large wheels are hand winding. The cans in the right foreground are for completed work

Above: As a man can be seen is operating a large guillotine, this is obviously a cutting room, but whether for cloth or card is hard to distinguish

Right: Men and women operating the very noisy braid machines. The workers became skilled lip readers after a time!

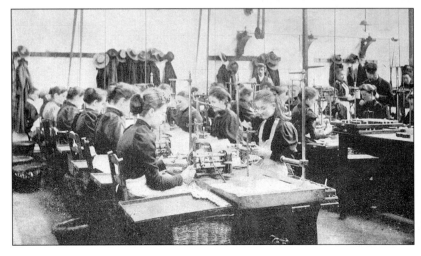

Left: The hand spooling department

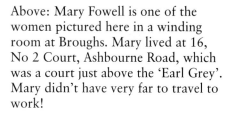

Above: Mary Fowell is one of the women pictured here in a winding room at Broughs. Mary lived at 16, No 2 Court, Ashbourne Road, which was a court just above the 'Earl Grey'. Mary didn't have very far to travel to work!

Middle: Mrs Annie Smith filling quills which were used on braid machines

Below: The Spooling department

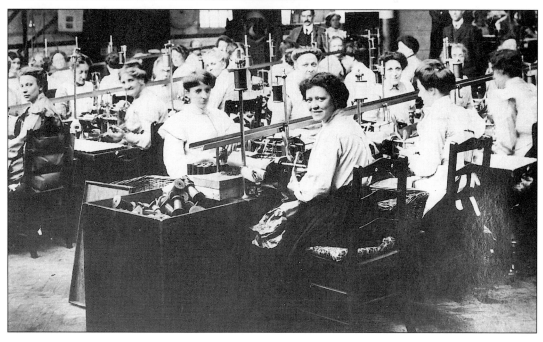

Above: Skilled Jacquard weavers. Harold D'Arcy and Harry Campion can be seen here hard at work

Left: Harry Campion operating a Jacquard loom which produced woven bookmarks, badges and hat bands

Below: Jacquard weavers. Basil Woodcock has his back to the camera. Others are Roy Randles; - Massey; Raymond Parr; ?; Edwin Cartledge; and John Dennis. In the background are two warps of a jacquard loom.

Above: A Coronation trip for Brough's employees. The lady in the front row with a case is Beatrice Robinson who worked at Broughs for over 50 years

Below: The window in this photograph can still be seen in Well Street just round the corner from Cross Street Mill. These Brough's employees pose formally, on the pavement outside their workplace

Woven silk bookmarks, all with a Royal theme,
produced by Brough, Nicholson and Hall on
Jacquard looms

In celebration
of the Centenary
of the
AMALGAMATED
SOCIETY OF
TEXTILE WORKERS
AND
KINDRED TRADES
AFFILIATED TO THE TRADES UNION CONGRESS
1871 - 1971
GEN. SECRETARY HERBERT LISLE J.P.

ESTABLISHED TO PROTECT NOT OPPRESS

More woven silk pictures:

Above left: "The Laughing Cavalier", a woven silk picture of a popular portrait

Above right: Another silk picture by G B Moroni. Although traditionally known as "The Tailor", the sitter's clothes are believed to reflect those of a member of the middle class

Far left: Salisbury Cathedral

Left: A book mark for the Centenary of the Amalgamated Society of Textile Workers and Kindred Trades

Left: A once familiar sight in Leek, one of Brough's delivery vans – the photograph was taken on 24th May, 1968

Below: An earlier Brough's mill in Union Street photographed in the early 1960s

Above: The Joiners' shop. The man sitting in the middle of the front row is George Clowes.
Jack Mathews is the man wearing a bowler hat

Below: An early view of the works; the department is not known

Above: In the canteen are Doris Clifford, Mrs Bode, Hilda Campion and Mrs Bishop

Two of the principal directors of the company; Left: John Hall, who for many years lived at Ball Haye Hall; Below: Joshua Brough

Erected in 1829 and used in the 1830s by the firm of Glendenning and Gaunt, who had 10 steam powered looms operating here in 1839. Power had previously been provided by Ball Haye Brook. According to Joseph Rider, who was an apprentice in the mill in 1831, there were 20 Dutch ribbon looms and one power loom in California Mill. William Stannard had the mill in the early 1880s and was still in business here in 1892. He lived at 7 Horton Street, a four-bedroomed property which still stands.

In 1920 William Pickford began to manufacture knitted goods in California Mill

Pinewood Fabrics
Limited

CALIFORNA MILL
HORTON STREET
LEEK, STAFFORDSHIRE, ST13 6EA

Telephone : LEEK **3153/4** (PBX)

✳

FOR THE ATTENTION
OF THE BUYER
SOFT FURNISHING DEPARTMENT

PATTERN
BOOK
RANGES
PRICE LIST

as at 1st JULY, 1970

and our

TERMS and CONDITIONS of TRADING

SAMPLES . . .

ON HANGERS

1¼ yards at Piece Price
also
Single Lengths (minus hanger)
at Piece Price Less 25%

. . . . . .

HANGERS — 3s. 6d. each

. . . . . .

BROCADE STANDS — 25 Guineas.

Height : 52 inches.
Length : 32 inches.
Width : 16 inches.
contains —
36 1¼-yard Hanging Lengths
of all Medium Priced Brocades
in our Range.

. . . . . .

DUPION/ACRYLIC STAND
Price : 35 Guineas.

contains —
1¼-yard Drapes of all our
Higher Priced Fabrics including
Dupions, Velours, Sheers,
Acrylics, Weaves.

— — — — — — — — —

N.B.— FOR EVERY END OF STOCK ORDERED
AT THE SAME TIME AS THE STAND IS
ORDERED, THE PRICE OF THE STAND IS
REDUCED BY 1 GUINEA.

Example —
8 Ends of Stock ; 1 Brocade Stand: £17. 17s. 0d.

— — — — — — — — —

Above: This view from Ball Haye Road on a postcard dated 28th March, 1906 shows several mills. The five storey California Mill dominates the scene with the factory of Clemesha Bros & Birch to the left. In contrast to the previous photograph California Mill still has its bell tower but not the fire escape, an obvious later addition. We are told that California Mill once had a weather vane with a fox on top. Apparently the fox symbolised the area where California Mill stands which was supposedly once known as Foxlowe

Left: Pinewood Fabrics from Amersham purchased California Mill in 1966 and carried out extensive internal alterations. Yvonne Porter shows off the firm's products

Pinewood Fabrics Staff at Christmas parties in the early 1970s

Above: In the middle of the photograph is Tom Cosgrove who worked at Clemesha's for many years as a fettler. During his time at Clemesha's he invented an oscillating bar which enabled the machine to make both circular and flat braid. Harold Baddeley a braid tenter can be seen on the right of the photograph. Also pictured are Harold Malkin and Josh Wardle

Left: Arthur Prime working on a braid head. He was one of a group of men known as speeders who set up the number of spindles needed to form the pattern

An evocative photograph by Arthur Goldstraw looking towards Park Terrace with the chimney of Clemesha Bros & Birch soaring above the factory. A silk mill on New Street was once worked by Gaunt and Wardle. In the 1830s Gaunt, Wardle and Walmsley were in business here. By 1872 Alsop Downes and Spilsbury occupied New Street Mill and manufactured silk thread there for many years. Alsop, Downes and Spilsbury employed hand loom weavers in the mill in 1900, they made dress fabrics and tailor serges. In 1907 Clemesha's moved into this mill

JUBILEE SOUVENIR
1873 === 1923

CLEMESHA BROS.
and BIRCH, Ltd.,
LEEK, England.

Above: A somewhat sanitized and imaginative drawing of the mills in New Street and Horton Street, occupied by Clemesha Bros and Birch. John Clemesha began his business in 1873 in a shade over three cottages, standing near to the White Lion in Ashbourne Road. Later joined by his brother William they established Clemesha Bros and moved into Wellington Street. Here they employed only a spooler, a winder and an errand boy. As the firm developed they moved into Shoobridge Street and then into London Mill. Increasing business demanded larger premises resulting in the move to the silk mills in New Street

Right: 'Ariel', the trade mark of Clemesha Bros & Birch Ltd

John Chapman Clemesha, the founder of the firm. Born in Preston in December 1849 and educated at Ackworth boarding school in Yorkshire, he came to Leek in 1873. In 1881 John was lodging at 4 Ball Haye Road and was described as a silk manufacturer employing 6 hands. When Clemesha Bros & Birch celebrated their Jubilee in 1923 John Clemesha was presented with a case of gold mounted Loewe briar pipes

Below: Employees and directors of Clemesha's celebrate Christmas. The year is not known, neither are the names

Above: Workers streaming out of Clemesha's, one suspects that they knew the photograph was to be taken as they are all dressed in their best! This ornate doorway can still be seen in New Street. Over 500 people worked for Clemesha's in Ariel and New Street Mills

Below: In July 1923 employees of Clemesha Bros & Birch Ltd left Leek railway station at 6.30am for an outing to Blackpool. After passing by Rudyard, through Macclesfield, Stockport, Manchester, Wigan, Preston and Kirkham they reached Blackpool at 9.30 am. After marvelling at the Tower and the Great Wheel, the 515 employees and directors met in the Indian Lounge at the Winter Gardens for luncheon

Finished garments manufactured by Clemesha's including scarves, ties, sweaters and cardigans

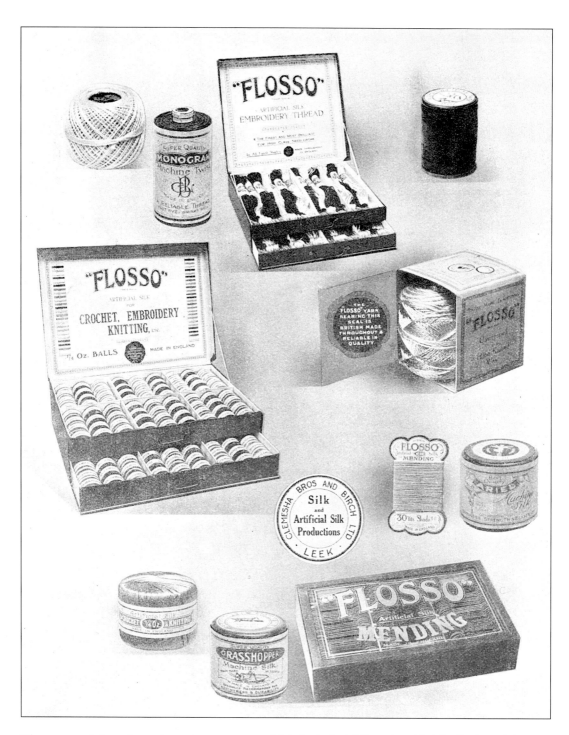

The range of threads made at the company which included 'Flosso' artificial silk thread for mending, knitting, emroiderery crochet. Also 'Grasshopper' machine silk and 'Monogram' machine twist

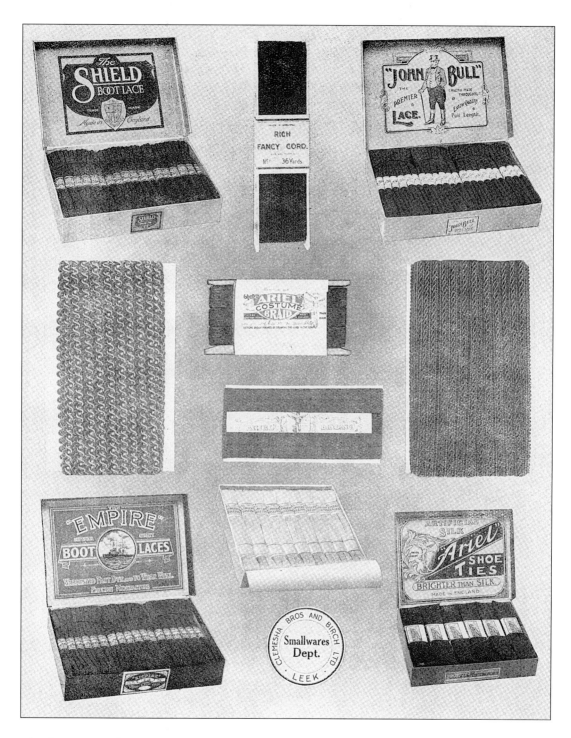

The famous 'Ariel' trademark is seen here on shoe laces and costume braid. Clemesha's also made 'Shield', 'Empire' and 'John Bull' laces together with other braids and trimmings

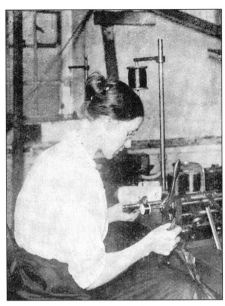

Above left: Carding silk and cotton mending
Above right: Hand spooling for net sewing silk

Above: Winding, spinning and throwing silks and artificial silks

Right: Automatic spooling for spun silks and mercerised cotton

Above: Hand filling for high class braids

Below: This machine produced the fleecy effect on all wool fabrics used for scarves, etc

Right: Mr P Clowes (referred to below)

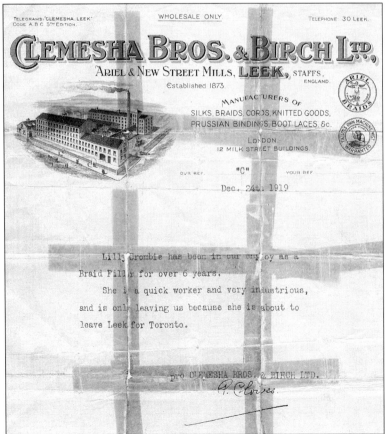

Left: A reference given in 1919 for Lilly Crombie who was about to leave Leek for Toronto. This testimonial is signed by Mr P Clowes who was manager of the braid department

Above: Working in the 'coat room' at Clemeshas. Included in this photograph are Mrs Wilson, Alan Matherson and Mary Heath. Clearly the ladies are working on other garments, not coats

Below: Smiling happily in the steam room at Clemesha's are Eileen Traynor, Nora Rogers and Barbara Ball

Pictured in this mill is E Stubbs who is measuring a length of strapping to edge a cardigan where it joins at the neck. The seam is flattened to prevent rubbing. Nelson Mills, home to C.W.S. Ltd, was formerly occupied by Leek Silk Twist Manufacturing Society Ltd who operated there during the first half of the 20th century. C.W.S. stood for Co-operative Wholesale Society

Above: There appears to be a conflict of view regarding the location of Daimler during the war. They were definitely at Stanards on Buxton Road, but were they also at Nelson Street? Daimler employees take a break for a work's photograph

C.W.S. LIMITED

WEAVING DEPARTMENT:
SAURER MECHANIC
GIRL for Making-up Labels.

KNITTING DEPARTMENT:
TRAINEE KNITTERS for Circular
Machines
BOYS for Pressing.

YOUTH for Yarn Stock Room
Permanent superannuated position.
First Class Welfare and Canteen facilities available.

Apply:
Nelson Mill, Nelson Street, Leek

Left: An advert for more employees in 1960s, from the *Leek Post & Times*

DAVENPORT, ADAMS
HOPE SILK MILLS, MILL STREET

6

George Davenport, a silk manufacturer, was in business in Mill Street by 1872 and by 1904 operated from Hope Silk Mills. In 1908 the company name had changed to Davenport (Geo), Adams & Co Ltd who were sewing silk manufacturers at Hope Silk Mill.

The mill pictured here bears a date of 1929 and the initials W.A and P.A. The smaller building to the left has been demolished together with the chimney but the stone column between the buildings still survives. Davenport Adams began with the manufacture of braid, sewing and embroidery silks but later began to make ladies' rayon and nylon underwear. They also produced knitwear and scarves.

On the ground floor, at the rear of the premises, was a dyehouse. Thus Davenport Adams was able to carry out everything on the site from processing and dyeing to the manufacture of the finished article

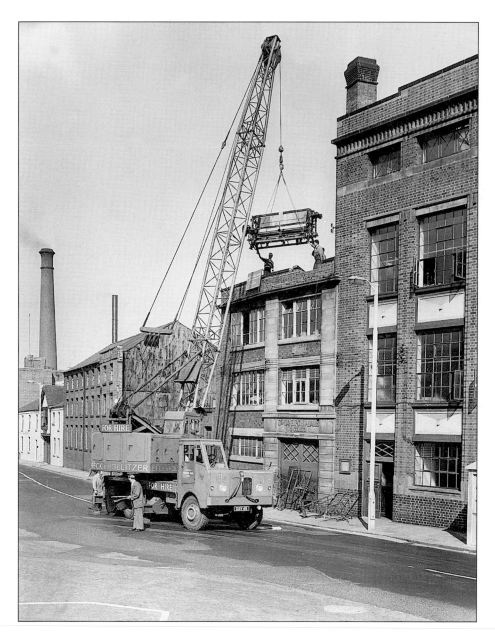

Left: In May 1959 Job Whites purchased Hope Silk Mills from Davenport Adams. Here (above) machinery is being moved into the mill. In 1991 Hope Mill had been empty for eight years and plans were proposed to turn it into flats. This did not happen and Hope Mill is now home to Supersports (Leisure Shirts) Ltd. The buildings to the left have been demolished

Above: Mr Joe Earls and Mr Coates, directors of Davenport Adams

Below: The dyehouse at the back of the mill. Note the jugs for mixing the dye and the dye baths

Above: The Reeling Embroidery Department

Below: The works from Belle Vue showing the three storey (to the left of the mill) extension which has now been demolished

Above: The knitting department with its long row of machines

Below: Solemn faced men in the braid department

Above: These long spinning and throwing machines seem to be tended by sole operatives

Below: Girls in the cutting room weilding scissors on cloth laid out on long tables

Above: Industrious ladies supervised by solemn faced men – before the days of equal opportunities!

Below: A galaxy of girls crowded together at their machines in the making up department

In this busy room girls examined finished articles, pressed them and then packed them into boxes

A view from Overton Bank looking towards the ruins of Britannia Mill in West Street. This mill was occupied for many years by Stephen Goodwin and Tatton Ltd., sewing silk manufacturers. Earlier photographs depict an extensive mill dominated by a huge chimney. Britannia Mill was formerly the premises of Ellis, Russell and Clowes, also silk manufacturers, who were in business here as early as 1825.

In 1831, 100 men and 8 women worked for Russell and Clowes, as the firm was then known, at this mill. A 12 year old child working half-time at Goodwin and Tattons silk mill in 1912 would be paid 2/6d a week for tagging laces. Half time meant half a day in the mill and half a day at school. There was a well beneath the chimney, as deep as the chimney was high. The mill was destroyed by fire in the early 1940s

Left: Stephen Goodwin lived at 47 St Edward Street in 1881. On the census of that year he is described as a silk manufacturer employing 50 people. The house in St Edward Street, now a dental practice, was home to Stephen, his wife and seven children. Four domestic servants were employed to look after the family. His son Arthur, then aged 17 and a silk warehouse man, later became the manager of Britannia Mill. The extensive range of products produced at Britannia Mill included sewing, embroidery and crewel silks, braids, bindings and cords

Right: Stephen Hall Goodwin, son of Stephen Goodwin was a silk broker in Britannia Mill. With him in this family group are his wife Rosamund and his children Nellie Rose and Stephen Arthur

Right: Ken Bowyer, the managing director of Gwynne & Co, manufacturers of sewing silks, mercerised cottons and pompoms. Gwynne & Co was situated in London Street, where the factory building still survives. It is now the premises of Odeon Antiques

Below: Ladies at work in Gwynne's. Winding frames can be seen in the right foreground while to the left are the pom-pom machines. Most of the pom-poms made at Gwynne's went to Job Whites for use on the countless bob-hats made there. One of the ladies in this photograph is Hilda Hancock

Classic & Hostess Gowns

Howards came to Leek during the Second World War when they relocated from London. First operating in All Saints schoolroom they later moved to Scola Mill behind Burgess' in Haywood Street. The company went into liquidation on 1st April, 1976. Employees of Howard's-made dressing gowns, housecoats and negligees. Their showroom in Regent Street, London was frequented by many famous people including well known actresses and even Princess Margaret

Left: An advert for Howard's products

Above: The Povey family, well known in Leek, came up from London with Howards. On the front row of this photograph are Emma Povey, head designer, her brothers David and Albert and her sister Frances

Below: Photographed here at a Christmas party at the 'Swan' in 1956 are:-
    Front row l-r: Frances Boden (nee Povey) a machinist, Emma Povey, manageress, Leopold Howard, Henry and Gordon Oakes, manager.
    Others include Nellie Harrison, Peggie Shenton, Mr & Mrs Albert Povey, Edna Kearton, Dorothy Boden, Wilfred and Ethel Brassington, Chris Bostock, Stan and Phoebe Murfin, Lana Harris, Irene Noakes, John Holmes, Gladys Bourne, Margaret Bradley, Brian Buxton, Graham Platt, Arthur Scragg, Fred Harrison and Edwin Bratt

Hugh Sleigh & Co occupied the mill on the corner of Shoobridge Street and Brook Street from the second half of the 19th century until the 1940s. Hugh Sleigh was a sewing silk manufacturer who lived in St Edward Street. As with other Leek mills this one was used by other businesses over the years. Gwynne & Co eventually bought Hugh Sleigh's mill and at one time Mason's took over the top floor. Hugh Sleigh lived at 64 St Edward Street, recently converted into a wine bar and restaurant

These photographs show different parts of the winding room at Sleighs

Above: Un the Winding room

Below: The warehouse in Sleigh's mill

The company started as a partnership between Herbert Trafford and Job White. Trafford and White operated in Victoria Mill, Ball Haye Road in 1909. They moved to Euston Mill in Wellington Street in 1911 and then to Compton Mill in 1912. The partnership between Trafford & White was dissolved in 1914 and William Davis joined White. The company became known as Job White in 1924 after Davis resigned. In the early years the company made braids and knitted ties and employed less than 50 people. Later they began to make garments, scarves and mufflers and the workforce increased to over 100. After the First World War, they began to make stockings with the brand name of 'Psychose' and also mens hose. In the 1930s they began to make hats and by the 60s were the largest producers of headwear in the country. Their brand name 'Moorcraft' became a household name. By the 1960s they employed over 600 people. In 1972, they were in difficulties and the administrator combined the activities of Wardle & Davenport and Job White & Sons, but this failed and both companies went into receivership within the year

Above: 'Moorcraft' was the brand name for Job White's knitted goods. Scarves, hats, sweaters, and ties are represented here

Below: Staff and agents celebrate Job White's 40th anniversary. Among those pictured are Billy Walwyn, Doris Swarbrook, Norma Talks, Mr & Mrs Ralph Baggett

Three views of the dyehouse
taken at different times

Above: The Winding Room

Left: Winding Machines

Below: The New Winding Plant in Compton Mill

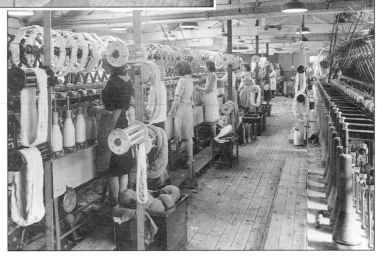

Above: The Warping Room

Right: The Warp Knitting
Plant using Raschel Looms

Below: Warping Machines

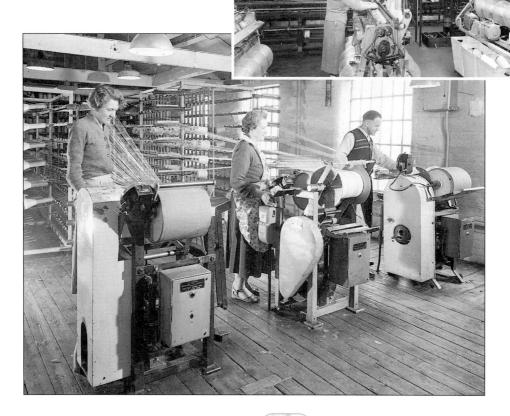

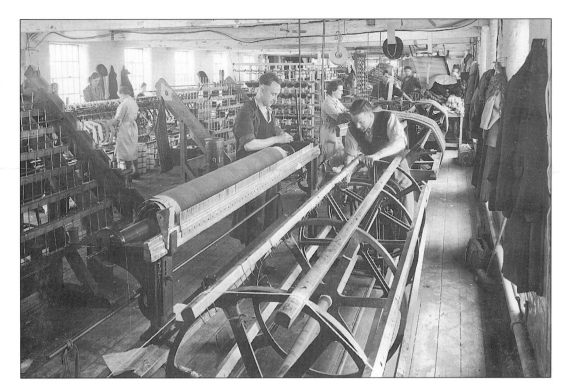

Above: Old warping machines in Compton Mill

Below: New warping plant

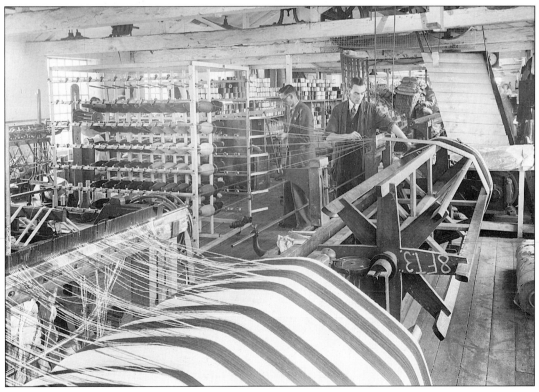

Above: Brushing

Right: The Knitting Department

Below: The circular knitting plant

Above: The Circular Knitting Plant

Left: The start of a new plant at Compton mill. On the left are Waga Bearded Needles and on the right is S.A.D Mellor Bromley machines

Below: Another Knitting Department this time using Flat knitting machines

Above: Raschel Looms in Compton Mill

Below: The circular knitting plant in Compton Mill

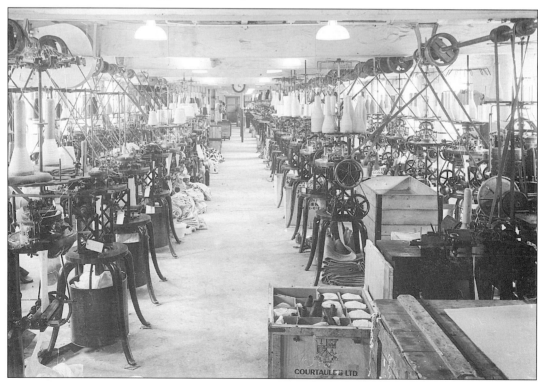

Above: Half-hose knitting Department

Below: Half-hose linking Department

Above: Braid tenters in the noisy braid department

Below: The Braid Machine Room

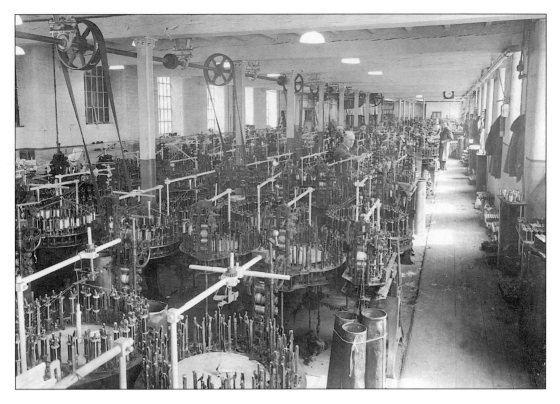

Above: The Braid Shed in Compton Mill

Below: The Braid Warehouse in Compton Mill

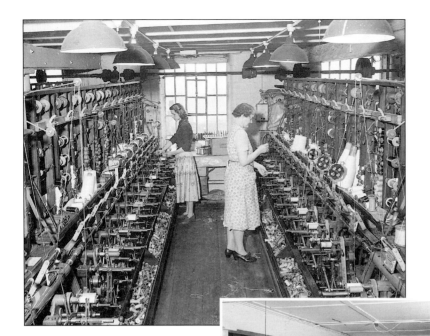

Above: The two ladies here are braid fillers

Right: Braid Picking and Making Up

Below: Old filling plant for braids in Compton Mill

Above: Steaming

Below: Rows of ladies making scarves and hats

Left: A busy room, on the right cotton is being wound. In the centre thread is being wound onto 'cops' and pom-poms are being made to the left. Pictured here are Hilda Hancock, Mrs Woodward and Mrs Goldstraw

Right: After the hats were made they were hand finished in this department. Piles of bobhats await pompoms

Below: Making up garments

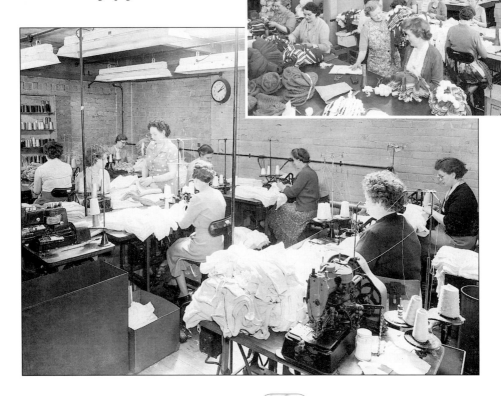

Making up scarves

Above: The machine room for headwear and gloves in Compton Mill

Below: Making up infant's wear

Above: The Making Up Department

Below: The Finishing Room

Above: Gloves by the hundred may be seen in the bottom making-up room

Below: The machine room in Compton Mill for headwear and gloves

Above: Fringing scarves
Below: The garment machine room in Compton mill

Above: Machine room for headwear and glove manufacture in Compton Mill Below: The hand knitting department at Moorland Mill, run by Moorland Handcraft Ltd, a subsidiary

Above: Tagging laces in Compton Mill

Below: Millinery sampling

Above: Cutting and packing scarves

Below: The Despatch Room

Above: Festooned with bunting, crowns and streamers as employees of Whites get into the festive Coronation spirit. Fifth from the left is Phyllis Biddulph (nee Pedlar)

Right: The Dyed Stockroom in South Street

Above: The Mechanics Shop

Below: The General Office

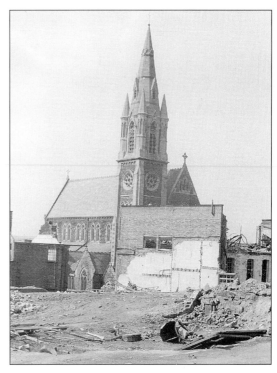

In 1964 a fire started in the dyehouse at Compton Mills, exploding chemicals caused a blazing conflagation which could be seen for miles around. Seventy five firemen battled for over two hours to control the flames. Police with loudspeakers organised the evacuation of over two hundred people from their homes in the vicinity of the mill. Hundreds of spectators converged on Compton to witness the fire and a wide area of the town was covered in smoke, soot and ashes. The photographs on this page bear witness to the devestation caused by the fire. The remains of the old mill were demolished together with surrounding cottages to open up the site

A new factory and admin block was built on the site of the mill destroyed in the fire at a cost of £300,000. Job Whites reopened in 1965 just one year after the devastating blaze. To mark this occasion directors of the firm were presented with silver ashtrays bearing the company's name and the employees had glass ashtrays with a picture of the new factory incorporated. This photograph was taken on the day when the new factory opened

Two further views of the re-opening

Above & below: The machine room in 1965

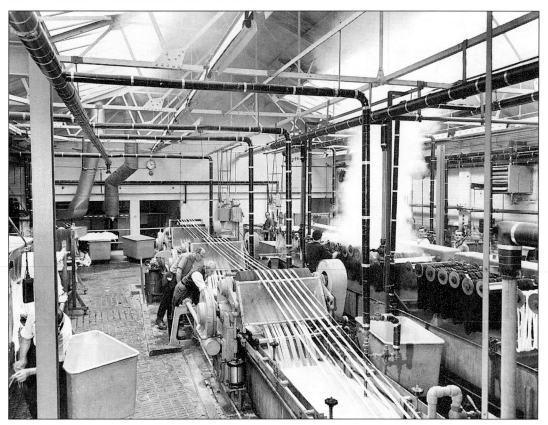

Above: The re-built dyehouse

Below: The re-built works following the fire. This photograph also shows quite a lot of other buildings which no longer exist. Copyright: Aerofilms

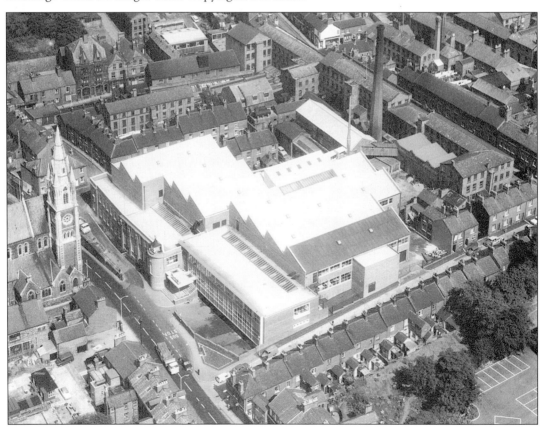

JOHN MASON & SON
SHOOBRIDGE STREET & LONDON STREET

Masons occupied the premises at the bottom of Shootbridge Street, once used by Hugh Sleigh & Co (see chapter 10). They now operate from London Mills in London Street

A Christmas party in the factory. Amongst the balloons, crackers, pickled onions and cakes are:- Glenys Owen, Julie Muir, Fiona ?, Gillian Fernyhough, Chris Unsworth, Jeanette Tart, Beryl Blore, Doreen Slack and Linda Jones

Left: In 1987 Mason's celebrated 50 years in the textile industry with a party at the Southbank Hotel. To remind everyone of the firm's origins in 1937 the employees were asked to attend in appropriate 1930s style attire

Right: Celebrating in style are design room staff from Masons.
Back row l-r: Beryl Bloore, Rita Hunter, Chris Unwin, Gillian Fernyhough, Chris Ryan, Julie Muir and Jeanette Tart.
Front row: Gill Hambleton, Glenys Owen

Left: An advert from the *Leek Post & Times* in may 1971

Above: Smiling young ladies proudly display the shield they won as winners of a Leek Carnival float competition

Below: Glasses of wine denote a celebration. All of these Mason's girls seem to be enjoying themselves – all except the girl wearing the hat who was to be married in a few days time!

Above: Sir Stanley Matthews with Mason's employees at a Christmas party in the 1970s

Left: Employees outside the factory. Masons Lingerie brand names included 'Lady Sylvia' and 'Cherita'. In 1971 the company acquired 'Eagle Mill' in Shoobridge Street for their cutting department and stock room

JOSHUA WARDLE
LEEKBROOK

A train passes under the bridge at Leekbrook with the Joshua Wardle site spreading out in the distance. Joshua Wardle started his business at Leekbrook in 1830, the address of the company in 1835 was given at Sheephouse Gate. It remained here until the business closed in 2002, although it contracted from the earlier premises, known as the Old Works, some years ago

Above: Joshua Wardle's Old Works in the 1920s. The Old Travellers Rest can be seen just in front of the work's chimney. Mrs Rogers who kept this inn was very kind to the men who worked in the boiler house. Ralph Fleming remembers how she would supply the men with pies at dinnertime. Nowadays the Traveller's Rest stands on the opposite side of the road

Below: Building the new works at Leekbrook in 1929. The girders for the new building were transported from Leek Railway Station on timber drags (drugs) pulled by teams of horses. Note the vehicle with solid tyres parked by the construction

Above: Huge amounts of water are needed for the dyeing industry and boreholes were sunk to access water supplies. Here a borehole is being sunk; unfortunately the water from this particular borehole proved to be too sandy and was never used

Below: Installing the new boilers in 1929. These were Lancashire boilers made in Manchester and they incorporated Bennis automatic stokers. The coal was taken up to a conveyor belt which fed hoppers which in turn supplied the boilers. Ash from the fire boxes was dropped into trucks and then taken away (see also photographs over page)

Ladders, pulley, ropes and cranes proliferate
as the new boilers are lifted into position

Above: A closer view of the Leekbrook works. All types of yarn were dyed here including a special range of black shades. 'Raven Black' and 'Blue Black Superior' became very well known. The special properties of the waters of the River Churnet contributed to the success of these shades and to the dyeing industry in Leek as a whole. Close-up views of this photograph may be seen on page 108

Below: One of the boilers is hoisted into position in the new works in 1929. This boiler bears the words 'Preston and Blackburn'

Above: Part of the process machinery in the New Works

Below: The scene at Leekbrook in recent years; sadly Joshua Wardle's is no more and the dyeing industry no longer continues its historic links with this site. The successors of Wardle's went into receivership earlier this year

Above: A presentation at the Old Works. Taking part in this happy occasion are Charlie Harrison, Frank Findler, Fred Mycock B.E.M., Norman Turner, Pat Charnock and Tom Wardle

Below: The Stocking Room at Joshua Wardle. The firm undertook the dyeing and finishing of hosiery. Pictured here are Nancy Tidmarsh, Gladys Harrison, Gladys Renshaw, Doreen Bird and Irene Nicholls

Above: A works dinner in the canteen.
Front row l-r: Joe Deakin, Mrs Thorpe, Mr Thorpe, Miss Oldman, Pat Charnock, Mary Charnock. Middle row l-r: Mrs Shackleton, Mrs K Balay, Nurse Woodward, unknown, Mrs Turner, Miss Turner. Back row l-r: unknown, John Balay, Len Shackleton, Norman Turner. John Balay, the managing director, masterminded the changeover from the dyeing of woven cloth to the dyeing of knitted fabrics

Below: Maintenance men pose at Joshua Wardle's Old Works. This photograph was taken by Jack Bagguley who was also among this group: Front l-r: Pat Charnock, Reuben Lowndes, Charles Harrison, Frank Findler, Fred Mycock, Harold Deaville, Ken Lovatt, Ralph Fleming, Teddy O'Brian, Fred Lowndes. Back row: l-r: Matt Foster, Ernie Brooks, George Morris, Alec Brown, Jack Bagguley, Eddie Pegg, Jack Brassington, Bill Pointon

Above: Finishing stockings in a room decorated for the 1937 coronation are Rosie Ward, Nancy Braddock, Eva Wright, Doris Fleet, Irene Nicholls, Winnie Woodward, ? Clowes, Ada Price, Olive Corden, Ivy Connor, Joan Pegg, Mary Simcox, Eva Alcock

Below: Many of Leek's large firms encouraged social and sporting activities as can be seen here in this photograph of Joshua Wardle's Sports Club in 1933.
Back row l-r: F Davenport, Mr Hambleton, Jack Thomas, Rafe Hammersley, George Bostock. Middle row: Harry Birch, ? Moss, Percy Williams, ? Dunkerley, Fred Boulton, Browhill, Billings, J Egerton. Front row: Johnson, Lomax, Shires, W C Charnock, Calvert, Dean, Edge, J Loton

Left: Joshua Wardle's badminton team Second from left on back row is Pat Charnock. Most of the names of this team are unknown, but two of the surnames are thought to be Fenton and Hemmings

Right: Joshua Wardle employees enjoying fun and games after a dinner dance at Rudyard. The lady on the right is Irene Fleming who is standing in front of her husband Ralph. The rather strained expression on Irene's face may be due to her desperately trying to hold a penny between her knees!

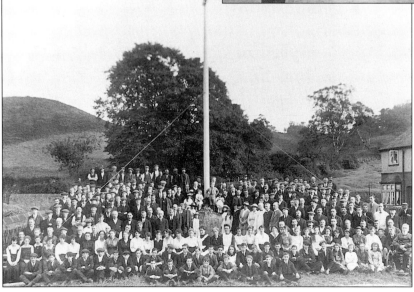

Left: Staff of the Old Works gathered around the War Memorial c. 1920. The memorial is situated in front of Bull Banks

Two views of dyers

Above: The Old Works in the 1950s

Below: The 1920s New Works photographed at the same time

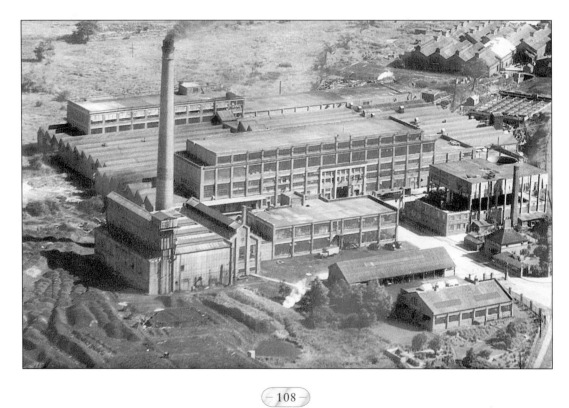

Inside Gordon Mill on Barngate Street in December 1915. Spun silk was first manufactured in Leek by William Watson & Co., in 1880. Spun silk thread was made from silk waste. Several local businessmen joined together to found the Leek Spun Silk Spinning & Manufacturing Co. One of these men was Thomas Wardle. In 1892 the company was operating in London Mills in London Street but in the early 1900s had moved to Gordon Mills in Barngate Street where they remained until 1958. Shortly afterwards 'Slimma' moved into the mill

Right: The only ladies whose photographs survive from their days at 'Leek Spun Silk'. Picking waste from left to right are: Alice Bullock, Mrs Hicks, Mary Naylor, Harriet Lovatt, Mrs Murfin, Mrs Wood and Mrs Penny

Above: Drawing and spinning machines in Leek Spun Silk. The same men are pictured here as on other photographs. Could it be they were posing when all the other workers were at home?

Below left: Twisting yarn for Leek Spun Silk in July 1917 are Charles Curson, Jim Fernyhough jnr, Jim Fernyhough snr, who was the engine man

Below right: The steam engine, also in 1917, with the same three men

This imposing factory, Waterloo Mills, was built in 1894 for William Broster and designed by James Gosling Smith. William Broster and Co manufactured sewing threads of pure silk together with cotton and rayon threads. In later years the business expanded to include bindings, ribbons, braids and elastics.

William Broster first operated from 'Big Mill' in Mill Street. For a time he also had a silk mill at Oakamoor in the 1850s. In 1953, William Broster and Co merged with Lux Lux Ltd and the factory began to produce underwear, lingerie and nightwear

Business boomed at Waterloo Mills in 1985 when Lux Lux employees pulled out all the stops to ensure that a £1/2 million order reached Debenhams stores on time. This new range of glamour wear was called 'Presence' and required yards of satin, lace, ruffles and feathers. The range included slinky 1950s style low-back nighties and cami-knickers!

Above: This photograph is believed to be of machinists in Broster's Waterloo Mills. The festive decorations and bunting would seem to indicate a royal occasion

Below: This photograph is from the 1970s and shows the design department staff

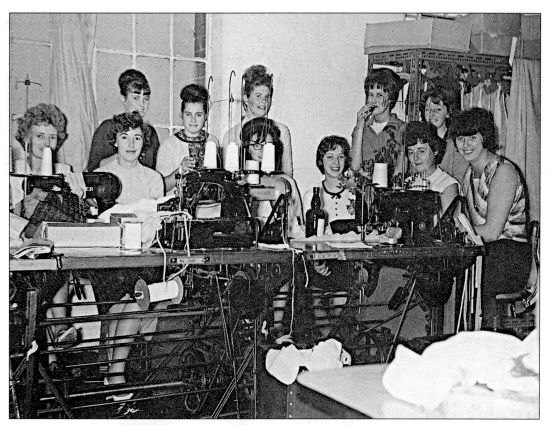

Both photo-
graphs: Lux
Lux design
department
in the 1960s

Above: Hard at work making up garments. Lux Lux for years did well out of orders for Marks & Spencers

Right: Staff in the early 1950s

Below: This is believed to have been staff from Lux Lux at a social gathering, probably in the late 1960s or a little later

Right: An advertisement from
a 1982 Leek Town guide

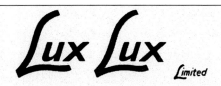

Lux Lux Limited

Registered in England 316909
Manufacturers of Ladies' Underwear & Slumberwear
WATERLOO MILLS : LEEK : STAFFS : Leek 383414

Lingerie and Light Clothing Manufacturers

Stocked by all the Best Lingerie Shops and
Departmental Stores throughout the Country

We employ mainly ladies operating a modern sewing
plant and usually have **Vacancies** for:
Experienced Overlockers and Machinists
Attractive working conditions and excellent wages
Subsidised Transport from most areas
Full Training given to young Ladies leaving School
and wishing to make a career in the Clothing Industry

Our Staff Store is open to Visitors
Waterloo Mills
Monday - Friday 10.15 a.m. - 11.45 a.m.
Frith Street Mill
Monday - Thursday .1.30 p.m. - 4.30 p.m.

Associated Companies in Leek
WILLIAM BROSTER & CO., WATERLOO MILLS, LEEK
GORT MANUFACTURING CO., LTD., FRITH STREET MILLS, LEEK
TELEPHONE: (All Three Companies) LEEK 383414

PARENTS AND SCHOOL LEAVERS
YOU ARE INVITED TO VISIT THE

Lux Lux

nightwear and leisurewear production units

WE CAN OFFER FULL TRAINING AS A

MACHINIST
OR
OVERLOCKER

in our recently established Training Centres

Opportunities are available in other sections of our production units
Come and see for yourself what we have to offer before deciding on your
career:—

* Excellent working conditions.   * Correct training by qualified instructors.
* Guaranteed wage during training.   * High piece work rates after training.
* 40 hour week.   * Three weeks' holiday.
* Canteen facilities with free drinks at breaks.   * Garments from the Cost Price Shop.
          * Transport provided to outlying districts.

CONTACT THE MANAGERESS AT EITHER UNIT . . . .
MRS. S. BROOKES   **MRS. E. REECE**
FRITH STREET MILL   **WATERLOO MILLS**
or
TEL. LEEK 3414

Left: Advert for Lux
Lux from the 1960s.
Many people will
remember Mrs
Reece at Waterloo
Mills and Mrs
Brookes at Frith
Street Mill. There
was no shortage of
jobs for young ladies
in Leek's thriving
textile trade

MAYERS
EUSTON MILL, WELLINGTON STREET

Mr Sampson Mayers founded this company in 1917. He first operated in the Tan Yard in Ball Haye Green with a couple of small knitting machines. During the 1920s, while still in Ball Haye Green, business was so bad that Mr Mayers was forced to give away his stock of rolls of fabric. The four storey Euston Mill was built for Brunt, Fynney & Roberts in 1853, but by 1912 was occupied by Trafford, White & Co. Some time later Mayers who made knitted fabrics for the medical trade, and for underwear, moved into Euston Mill

Right: In 1979 the Wellington Street premises was reduced to a pile of blackened rubble when fire swept through the buildings. People were evacuated from the nearby houses as firemen battled to control the flames. The Wellington Pub is on the right

Left: This scene is from Strangman Street, with Wellington Mills on the left

This page & opposite top: The works had to be demolished following the fire. A row of bungalows now stand on the site of the former mill. The houses in the above photograph are numbers 1 to 11, Cruso Street

Below: Mayers' employees at a Christmas party in the Hotel Rudyard
Front row: Audrey Foster, Doreen Tidmarsh, Annie Frith, Mavis Wragg. Second row: Lilian West, Sheila Mayers, Annie Mayers, Mr & Mrs S Mayers, Mr & Mrs Sidney Knight. Others include: Ken Worthington, Betty Keates, Mrs Gold, Peggy Shingler, Ada Foster, Leah Yates, Kate Murfin, Elsie Large, Rose Stonier, Grace Yates, Jean Clews, Jack Bratt, Reg Hollinshead, Charlie Waterhouse, Joan Harvey, Bernard Trafford, Olive Lunt, Ivy Banks, Arthur Graham, Jean Barlow, Harry Bratt, Bill Bowyer, Florrie Newsome, Jimmy Hathersall, Bill Greenwood and Bill Maycock

Above: Long tables and festive fayre as Mayers' employees celebrate at Rudyard. In the foreground are Doreen Tidmarsh, Jean Clews, Vera Robinson and Alan Clews
Others include: Bill Bowyer, Russell Bowyer, Cyril Rowley, Alan Foster, Marion Hancock and Stuart Bowyer

Below: Another Christmas party for Mayer's employees

Right: From left:
Mrs Owen, Alan
Clews, Jean
Clews, Enid
Rushton, Phyllis
Bowcock, Bill
Owen, Dorothy
Spooner. The
lady at the back
is Annie Frith

Below: Sampson Mayers' workforce on a day trip to Leamington in about 1948.
The three young boys at the front are Keith Worthington, John Rider and Keith Dale. Among
others on the photograph are Jack Bratt, Violet Bratt, Derek Bratt, John Bratt, Harry Bratt,
Mr & Mrs S Mayers, Mr Knight, Roger Knight, Mr & Mrs Ken Worthington, Charlie
Robinson, Vera Moss, Jimmy Hathersall, Mr Wilshaw, Beryl Wilshaw, Ted Clarke, Mr Green-
wood, Mrs Keates, Frank Keates, Grace Yates, Joan Clarke, Dennis Fisher, Ethel Fisher, Reg
Hollinshead

Two more views of Mayer's annual Christmas party, the dates are unknown

Mr Arthur Fogg, one of the directors, photographed in the early 1930s. William Milner first started in business in Union Street where he was a sewing silk manufacturer. The company moved to Langford Street, where knitted goods were made, remaining there until about 1958. Shortly afterwards the Victoria Manufacturing Company moved into the mill

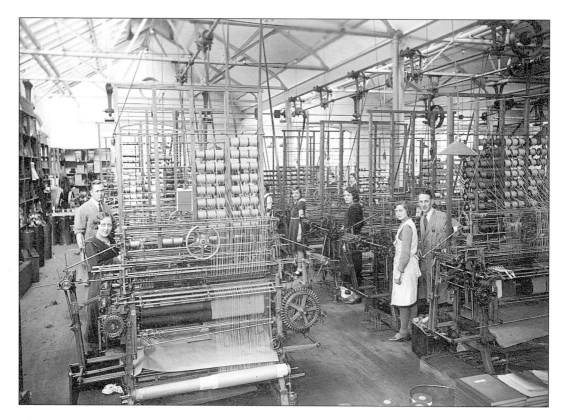

Above: Weaving looms in Milners, Ethel Grindey is the lady in the light coloured overall

Below: Standing in serried lines are Milners employees who operated the knitting machines

Above: Braid tenters at Milners

Below: Rows of winding machines and lines of young ladies

Left: The making-up room

Right: One of the men pictured here is Harold Grindey. As part of his job he weighed finished braid in order to calculate an employee's pay

Left: The warehouse

Above: Mountford Johnson manufactured scarves, headwear and babywear at their New Grange Mill premises. This photograph dated circa 1948 shows a works Christmas party. In the group of people enjoying good food and wine are Elizabeth McIntyre, Hilda and George Oultram, Mr Warrington, Mrs Johnson, Mrs Bob Bailey and Mrs Findler

Left: 'Cosiworn' was the brand name of goods manufactured by W Mountfort Johnson & Co. In 1966 this thriving company was advertising for examiners and overlockers in their headwear and scarf departments and machinists for their babywear department. In May 1982 60 firemen battled a blaze at New Grange Mills, now occupied by J S Knitwear. Thirteen fire appliances attended the fire which destroyed both machinery and stock. The works faces Prince Street

ALEXANDRA MILL

This silk mill stands on the corner of Queen Street and Earl Street. Thomas and Vernon Myatt, sewing silk manufacturers, were in business here from at least 1872. The Myatt family were closely associated with the Alexandra Football Club fondly known as 'Leek Alex' and with the Alexandra Boys Club which provided leisure time activities for Leek's young men. In 1964 the wrapper and box division of Adams Foods Ltd moved into the former silk mill. Today, Mr J Hartley has planning consent to establish a retail warehouse and discount store here

A view looking up Buxton Road looking past the 'Royal Oak' towards Premier Dyeing and
Finishing Co. Ltd

The 'Premier' building on the corner of Buxton Road and Portland Street North. The Premier company was established c. 1912 and developed the dyeing and finishing of silk, acetate and viscose rayon. Thousands of pieces of cloth were able to be dyed each week including jappes, satins and crepe-de-chines. The dyeing industry requires plentiful amounts of water and this was supplied by the companies own wells bored hundreds of feet into the ground

Above: The Buxton
Road frontage

Left: Many Leek textile
firms took part in the
annual Leek carnivals,
decorating lorries and
dressing in colourful
garb in order to parade
through the town. Here
are 'Premier' employees
on their decorative
float at one such
carnival

Above: A close-up of part of the Buxton Road frontage

Below & opposite: A selection of vehicles used over the years by the Premier Dyeing and Finishing Co. to transport fabric. In 1960 'Premier' became part of the Courtaulds group. Then in 1984, ten of the company's employees purchased the business in a management buy-out and the Leek Dyeing and Finishing Company was formed

Left: A staff Christmas party with Dave Smith, Jean Bode, Ronnie Bode, Tom Smith, Agnes & Ken Smith, Carol & Brian Goldstraw

Below: George Turner's retirement presentation: Nancy West, Graham Johnson, Ray Walters, David Belfield, Stephen Bayley, Ian Leek, John Macheter, Steve Brookes, Ron Mellor, Harry Pickering, Peter Morgan, George Murfin, Don Harris, George Turner, Alan Hill, Gerald Meakin, Clint Williams, Charlie Brough, John Pitcher, John Bradbury, Barry Astles, Peter Millward, Marjorie Sharrocks, Jean Bode, Christine Sales, Maureen Whiston

Above: Harry Lacy's retirement presentation with Richard Fowler, Brian Chapman, Joan Guderis, Ena Ainsworth, Mick Belfield, Don Harris, Annice Perkin, David Belfield, Joan Brown, Jean Bode, Harry Lacey, Margaret Dawson, Brenda Mellor, Maureen Whiston, Margie Sharrocks, Christine Sales, Les Emery, Charlie Brough, John Pitcher, John Salt

Below: Jean Bode ready for a work's party, seen in the Examining Room

PRETTY POLLY HOSIERY MILLS LTD
BUXTON ROAD

21

This mill was in Buxton Road just above the junction with Shirburn Road. The building still stands and since the beginning of this year has been used by Cavendish Windows and Conservatories. Prior to this it was used by the Pentecostal Church.

Pretty Polly manufactured fully fashioned nylons and were established in Buxton Road by 1929. In later years, Alberton Ltd were the occupiers of Pretty Polly Mills.

This photograph, dated 1929, shows members of the Pretty Polly swimming club at the old baths in Derby Street

Below: Back Row left to right: Mr and Mrs Salt (caretakers at the baths), Brenda Turner, Alice Savage, Ada Barlow, Hilda Tatton, Alice Burnett, Florrie Mellor, Elsie V Brocklehurst, ?. ?, ?, Ada Sharpe., May Hill, Elsie Bradley, ?

Front Row right to left: Nancy Crutchley, Florrie Goodfellow, Becky Dale, Gladys Dale, ?, Betty Mellor, Edna Flower, Gladys Gittens, ?, ?, Ethel Bloore, Lily Messham, Phyliss Messham, May Poole, Lottie Kennerley

Sir Thomas Wardle was the son of Joshua Wardle and was knighted in 1897. He purchased the Hencroft works on Abbey Green Road in 1872. In 1881, his son Arthur joined the business. A major expansion scheme began in 1938, including some of the buildings fronting Macclesfield Road. Bridge End dyeworks was acquired in 1956 from Brough, Nicholson & Hall and became the home of Leek Chemicals, which was acquired by Coutaulds in 1967 and later the whole firm was merged with Courtaulds. The creative talent of Sir T & A Wardle revolutionised the dyeing industry in late Victorian times and this has been documented elsewhere. Sir Thomas died in 1909. He lived in St Edward Street and at Swainsley Hall. He was part owner of Leek Spun Silk Spinning & Manufacturing, which spun silk from silk waste, an innovation first introduced by Wm Watson & Co.

Sir T & A Wardle was the largest production site in the town, extending to 52 acres, with its own sportsground and pavilion. It used 2 million gallons of water a day from the River Churnet; the water being filtered, softened and treated for use in dyeing.

There was a 4MW electricity load to the factory with a 11,000 volt supply from the Midlands Electricity Board. Its output required a fleet of 22 lorries for distribution. The whole site was self contained – even down to having its own fire brigade

Below: The near building housed automatic steam printing machines and was built c.1947-48. The three storey building was built c.1938 as two storey, being extended upwards about eleven years later. The top floor housed 50 feet long printing tables shown on p143

Above: The Macclesfield Road frontage c. 1960s

Below: A view of the works in 1974 from the valley side. A new sewage plant is being installed in the foreground

Examining printed cloth
(above) prior to despatch
(middle and bottom) in the
1960s

Above: A very old dyeing barque still in regular use in the 1960s made in the joiner's shop in the 1930s. This was used for rope dyeing, with the cloth sold in an "endless rope"

Below: Hand screen printing on 50 feet long tables with Eddie Stonehewer on the right. There were eight of these tables in use until the early 1960s. A 50 feet length was a piece and two pieces = one lump!

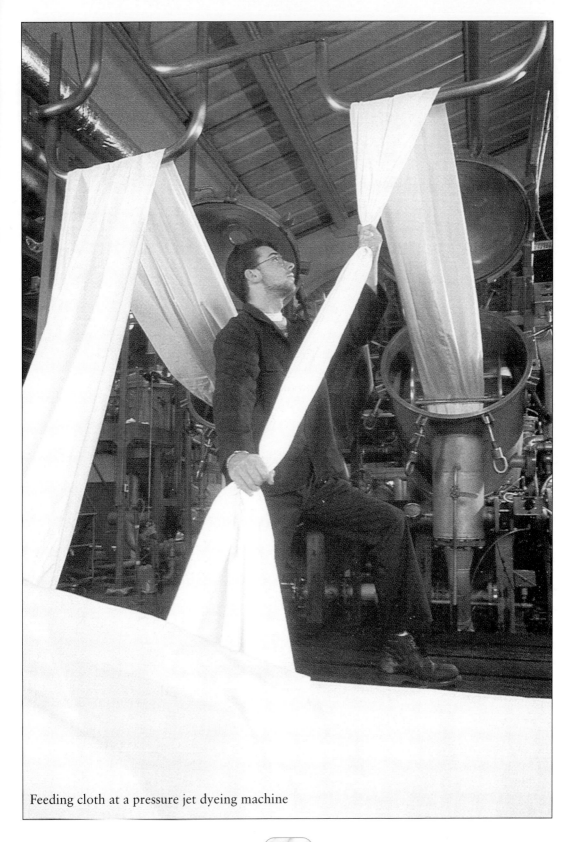

Feeding cloth at a pressure jet dyeing machine

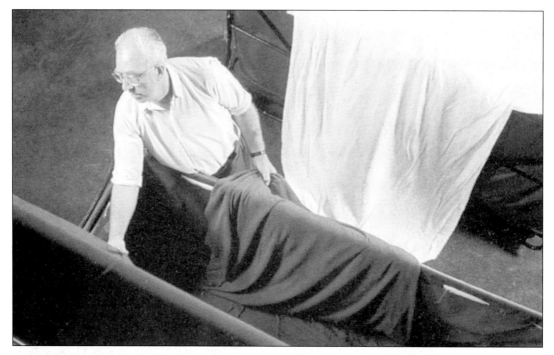

Above: A photograph from the company's last publicity brochure

Left: A view in the dyehouse showing the machinery for washing and desizing cloth prior to dyeing

Above & middle: Another desizing machine, purchased from Japan

Below: Shrinkwrapping machinery provided added protection before the rolls of cloth were despatched

Modern machinery and technical innovation remained at the forefront of company policy but external industrial pressures eventually saw the demise of the company which, under Sir Thomas Wardle, had revolutionised the dyeing industry of this country in late Victorian times

SIR THOMAS AND ARTHUR WARDLE LIMITED
COMMISSION DYERS, PRINTERS AND FINISHERS
CHURNET WORKS, MACCLESFIELD ROAD, LEEK

PRESERVING A LINK WITH FIRM'S 1881 FOUNDATION

A LINK with the first dyehouse bearing Messrs. Wardle's name?

This stone carved figure of a dyer was found in the old dyehouse, whitewashed over and director Mr. J. S. Gregory asked Messrs. Trentham's if they could get it out and incorporate it in the new premises. This was done, the stonework restored to its original colour and now it is inset in the wall at the dyehouse entrance.

Just how old it is and how it came to be carved, no one seems to know but the general belief is that it dates back from the start of the firm in 1881. Whatever its history it is still symbolic in 1966 of the industry which goes to make up today's production output.

£1m. EXPANSION PROGRAMME WILL HELP GIVE LEEK FIRM THE LARGEST INDEPENDENT DYEWORKS ACREAGE IN THE BRITISH ISLES

THE EXPANSION PROGRAMME of Sir Thomas and Arthur Wardle Limited, Churnet Works, Leek, commenced way back in 1938 but it is in the last six years that this busy works has really begun to grow visibly.

In those six years over £1,000,000 has been expended on capital projects, including £300,000 for the present year, ending December 31.

The policy of the Board of Directors is a simple one — earn enough to expand, then expand enough to earn more — a progressive and continuous business cycle which has, as its objective, establishment of the biggest acreage of dyeing, printing and finishing works in the British Isles, with a straight-through production unit which has already speeded up the flow of orders through the works, ensuring that the firm maintains its customers' goodwill and its own place as leaders in the processing of dyeing and — or printing of fabrics of all natural and man-made fibres and mixtures.

Early building developments were the commencing of what is now a vast, well organised grey warehouse, in 1938: followed after the war by a section of the finishing room and the opening in March, 1954, of the extensive inspection and despatch department.

It was, however, through the advent of the Cotton Industrial Act, of 1959, that the firm was able to move ahead in a big way, because the Act gave a much needed fillip to progressive firms like Sir Thomas and Arthur Wardle Ltd. who were prepared to modernise and expand, 25 per cent grants being available for purchase of new plant equipment.

Since that time the firm has continued to expand through its own earned capital, G. Percy Trentham Ltd., of Longton, having the contract for more buildings in which have been — and are being — installed the latest dyeing, printing and finishing plant on the British and Continental markets, with the result that today the works cover some 30 acres — with ample land for further expansion.

The Directors have just issued their interim report for the year ending December 31, 1966, announcing an interim dividend of 5 per cent, less tax. Group profits for the first six months, before deductions, totalled £216,760, compared with £197,358 for the first half of 1965, and £157,373 for the corresponding period of 1964.

Last year pre-tax Group profits rose by no less than 33 per cent. Issued ordinary capital in this public company is given as £544,000.

Each year shows a steady growth in the firm's traditional business and the Board anticipate that, subject to national and international conditions, this progress can be maintained and that with their workers' inherent skill, coupled with the most up-to-date equipment and lay-out in the country, augmented by further outlay of capital, Sir Thomas and Arthur Wardle Ltd. can continue to command a good share of the ever-expanding textile trade, both woven and knitted, in the large and comprehensive range of dyed and printed piece goods

'Post and Times' Special
Industrial Supplement
Thursday, September 8, 1966

The Leek Post & Times announces a £1m expansion programme in 1966

Above: Spontaneous combustion over a weekend destroyed this stock, but not the building. The warm material heated instead of cooling, showing how easy fires started in the town's textile mills

Above & right: The arrival of a new Richards
& Westgarth boiler in 1975, with a capacity of
40,000 lbs of steam per hour. Four of these
were installed to replace the old Lancashire
boilers, which raised 10-12,000 lbs of steam
each in comparison

Opposite bottom: Installing the leader cloth
prior to production for a new continuous
printer (left) with the machine in operation
later (right)

Below: Vic Porter removing ash from one of the
old Lancashire boilers prior to their replacement in 1975

Above: A visit by Rt. Hon. George Brown (MP for Belper) in c.1970. He was a director of the main board of Courtaulds, who owned Sir T & A Wardle Ltd. From l-r are: Harry Bellis (Technical Director); J W Reeves (Man Dir.,); G Imber (Print Dir): G Brown, MP; F Bode (Finance Dir.,); (?); John H Oliver (Chief Engineer); Ian Swarbrook; M Whitehurst: B West (in front); John Reeves; G Gwite; G Lees; Peter Rowan; George Feather (Finishing Room Dir.,); F Birtwhistle (Dyeing Dir.,): N Granger (Office Manager); (?); H Harrison (Foreman Engineer); - Samuels

Below: Following World War II, many iron or steel chimneys had rusted badly resulting from condensation caused by imposed lower firing temperatures. This shows such a replacement at the Churnet Works in August 1949. Here, a 130 feet high chimney is being winched up manually to sit on a plinth perhaps ten feet tall. Theoretically simple, it involved huge amounts of cable in tension as the chimney slowly lifted off the ground. The only question unanswered is how the man sitting on the rising chimney got off it! The chimney was built by Foster, Yates & Thom of Blackburn

Slimma took over the Leek Spun Silk Mill in James Street c.1958. James Street at that time was bordered by allotments. Seven years later Slimma built a new factory and office block on the corner of Barngate and James Street

Above: Gordon Mills which were later extended, see page 151

Vacancies at 'Slimma' in the mid-1960s when business was booming. Three hundred people worked in the factory which had cutting rooms, stock rooms, a warehouse, pressers, machinists and offices. Cathryn Walton, co-author of this book, worked as a comptometer operator in the wages office at this time. The girls were on piecework and sent up to the office tickets which showed the number of minutes taken to complete a procedure on the production line. A sound knowledge of decimals was needed to operate the comptometer and so calculate an employee's wages. Naturally severe displeasure would be expressed if you got it wrong.

Although Slimma started with a range of 'feminine slacks' they soon introduced skirts, beachwear and co-ordinated separates. These garments were sold all over the country in multiple stores and in mail order catalogues.

Slimma also had markets for their clothes in Europe, Scandinavia and the Middle East.

Slimma clothes were up-to-the-minute, trendy and fashionable in the 60s. Employees were able to buy garments at reduced prices in special sales held in the canteen. Cathryn once thought she was the "bee's knees" in a purple paisley patterned trouser suit. This colourful outfit had purple corduroy on the shoulders and flared trousers. A peaked cap in paisley pattern with purple corduroy beck completed this ensemble. Truly an awesome sight!

In 1981 ladies from 'Slimma' in Leek were in Harrod's London store. They were demonstrating how Slimma reversible skirts were made up. At this time 'Slimma' was thriving with a turnover exceeding £2 million. Over 72% of their designs were exported to France, Italy, Germany and the Scandinavian countries

Above: The former 'Slimma' despatch warehouse on the corner of Sneyd Street, occupying the site of the old Co-op bakery

Below: The 1965 extension on the corner of James Street and Barngate Street

TELEPHONE NOS. LEEK { 680 681 682

TELEGRAMS: STANNARD·LEEK

ESTABLISHED 1845

WILLIAM STANNARD & C^O L^{TD}
SILK MANUFACTURERS

SEWING SILKS
ARTIFICIAL SILKS
MERCERISED YARNS

BLOUSE &
GOWN SPECIALISTS

WHOLESALE AND SHIPPING ONLY

LEEK
STAFFORDSHIRE

PRINCESS HOUSE
EAST CASTLE ST., W.I.
PHONE 1966 MUS.

YOUR REF_____

OUR REF___ MJ ___

William Stanard was a silk manufacturer in London Street in 1872. He moved to California Mill in the 1880s and was still there in 1892. During the early years of the 20th century William Stannard & Co Ltd occupied a mill in Brook Street. About 1927/8 the glass and concrete factory in Buxton Road was erected and the company established there. Several hundred people were employed in the factory engaged in the manufacture of sewing threads including 'Shirlastic' elasticated thread. However the main product was ladies frocks and blouses which were sold all over the country to customers including C & A Modes. The workforce was made up of girls from Leek, the surrounding villages and the Potteries. Fleets of buses brought in the girls who lived out of town. Shown here is the company's letter head showing their Buxton Road factory

Right: During the war Stannard's Buxton Road Mill was taken over by the Daimler Co to supplement their war production. Stannards relocated to a room in Standard Knitting Co. at the top of Ball Haye Green, a room for the thread department in Milner's factory in Barngate Street and to Park Mills in Nelson Street. As this advertisement tells us, the registered office of William Stannard & Co Ltd was at Park Mills in Nelson Street. During the war Stannards made anti-gas capes of oiled cotton and Stannard/Bunyan irrigation envelopes used for the treatment of burns. It was Commander Bunyan RN, a surgeon, who jointly developed the idea for the envelopes with William Stannard. After the war, the Buxton Road factory was sold to William Tatton & Co.

William Stannard & Co. Ltd.
&
Stannards (Oiled Silks) Ltd.

Registered Offices:
PARK MILLS, NELSON ST., LEEK, Staffs.

Works:
PARK MILLS, NELSON ST. ⎫
LANGFORD STREET ⎬ LEEK, Staffs.

SQUARE MILL, STRINGER ST. ⎫
RELIANCE MILL, WALLEY ST. ⎬ BIDDULPH, Staffs.
BROOK MILL, STATION RD. ⎭

Showroom:
PRINCESS HOUSE, EASTCASTLE STREET, LONDON, W.1

Telephones:
Leek 680-1-2.   Biddulph 2224-5-6.
London Museum 1968

Manufactures:
Sewing Cottons and Silks, Mending, Embroidery and Knitting Yarns. Frocks, Blouses, etc. Oiled Silks, Nylon and Cotton Piece Goods. Mackintoshes, Pixie Hoods, etc.

C. PLANT
BARBARA ZAC.

Below: A group of young errand boys working at Stannards pose pensively in 1939. Anticlockwise from top are: Derek Evenson, Les Byatt, Roy Stafford, Harold Dale, Don Woodcock and Basil Tomkinson

Above: William Stannard's cricket team.
Back row: Norman Piercy, George Oultram, John Crossley, Norman Keates, Clyde Bates, ?, ?.
Front row: Les Hackney, Harold Dale, Billy Morley, Bill Bibby

Left: Office equipment of yester-year as represented by this Burroughs accounting machine used at Stannards. It looks much more complicated than a computer!

WILLIAM **TATTON** & CO. LTD.
BUXTON ROAD, LEEK

This expanding Company processing and dyeing man-made fibres invite young men and women to come and discuss careers in the industry

All successful applicants will be considered for a place on the specially devised and carefully supervised Management Training Scheme which includes full time and part time courses at various educational establishments as well as extensive internal training.

Apply to Mr. M. Smeaton, Buxton Road, Leek

MANAGEMENT TRAINEES

Work Study, Production Management, Production Planning, Accountancy, Distribution Management.

JUNIOR TECHNOLOGISTS

Fibre Chemistry, Fibre and Fabric Technology, Development, Quality Control, Value Analysis, Customer Liaison.

COMMERCIAL ASSISTANTS

Home and Foreign Sales, Sales Accountancy, Regional Commercial Management.

CRAFT APPRENTICES

Mechanical, Electrical and Electronic Engineering and Maintenance.

MACHINE OPERATORS

Dyeing and Processing — high bonus earnings and other benefits.

William Tatton used the factory in Buxton Road for his head office. An extensive addition was added at the rear of the factory. 100,000 ft of floor space was added and a uptwisting plant was installed together with machinery for processing nylon high-twist yarns for hosiery manufacturers. The machinery ran night and day for twenty two years

Above: Business was booming in Buxton Road as this advertisement for various employees demonstrates

Above: The coronation arch on Buxton Road by Byrne's Garage, in 1953. The decorations on Tatton's factory can also be seen through the arch. These elaborate, decorative and imaginative arches were designed by Arthur Littlewood

Below: A Berliner uptwisting machine in Intex Yarns on Buxton Road. The Tattons factory on Buxton Road was taken over by Intex Yarns in the early 1970s. This photograph was taken shortly before the devestating fire in May 1975. The call to the fire brigade was made at 26 minutes past midnight and the first water ladder arrived three minutes later. Three hundred workers were evacuated from the building in minutes but the factory was destroyed, the blaze causing an estimated £5 million of damage. The fire spread rapidly even though seventy firemen fought the blaze

Above: A Tatton's cricket team in the 1950s. Among others on the photograph are Horace Moreton, Len Sheldon, Basil Stafford, Alan Clews, Bernard Mansfield, Ian Mitchell, Philip Bowcock, Derek Edge, Stan Lockett and Mr Barnett

Right: An advert from the 1960s

Pictured here at a Christmas dinner dance at the Town Hall in 1956 are Maxwell Alexander Tatton, chairman and managing director of Tattons, with his wife, and some of his staff

In 1872 Joseph Gould was a silk manufacturer here, he was replaced by T Flanagan and Company who manufactured thread here for many years. In 1911 the Victoria Manufacturing Company was formed at the time when artificial silk or rayon became popular. Victoria Manufacturing made knitted ties, scarves, cardigans, jumpers and dresses. The four storey mill was destroyed by fire in 1945 together with all the machinery and stock. This site, next to the Park Tavern, is now occupied by a Medical Centre

William Hill was a sewing silk manufacturer in Wellington Mill from at least 1892 until the premises were built in Burton Street in 1923. In Burton Street, the firm manufactured silk and cotton threads plus synthetic fibres

Above: The works as seen today

WILLIAM HILL & CO.
SEWING SILK
MANUFACTURERS

Registered Brands:
" STAR," " EXCHANGE," " AIM-HIGH."

Manufacturers of:
Tailors' Raven Sewing Silks, Tailors' Cloth Sewing Silks, Military Sewing Silks, Glove Silks, Button-hole Twists, 1 and 2-oz. Reels, Tailors' Legee Twists, Machine Sewing Net, and Spun Silks for Clothing Manufacturers.

Manufacturers of:
Machine Sewing Net and Spun Silks specially prepared for Boot and Shoe Manufacturers, 12 - yards Button - hole Twists, 50 - yards Machine Sewing Silks and Mercerised Cotton Yarns on reels or cops.

Star Silk Mills
BURTON STREET, LEEK
South African Representatives: Messrs. Brown & Walton Ltd.
Capetown—96 Long Market Street.   Telephone 2-5246.
Johannesburg—121 President Street.   Telephone 4735.

Right: An advert for the company's products

Above: Benjamin Hill, son of William Hill, managing director of the family business

Below: Pictured in the warehouse at Star Mill are Harold Hill, Arthur Hill, Vera Cooper, Arthur Worthington and Ken Bowyer

Above: This photograph was taken in a long shed at the back of Star Mill. The men here are hand silk twisters. The twister turned the wheel while the young twister's helpers carried the thread on bobbins to the end of the shed. There they passed the thread through hooks and returned to the twister, he then turned his wheel and on the way the twist was put into the silk thread. The wheels can be seen at the back and the boy who is a twister's helper can be seen in the middle of the photograph, holding the row of bobbins. The boys ran back and forth across the long room all day, an estimated 20 plus miles a day, they are sometimes collectively known as the Staffordshire Trotters. The boy sitting on the left is Cyril Sheldon, helper to his father, who is standing behind him. The young boy sitting on the right is Fred Hackney

Below: The winding room. Marie Sheldon is the lady centre front, both her father and her brother also worked for Hills

Above: These men are silk pickers, they patiently examined the silk thread after it had been uptwisted, picking off any waste material. Two of the men here are Harold Rhead and Billy Malkin. Ken Bowyer recalls that some of these men did this job for years

Below: In this room three bobbins of silk were used to make one thread. This process is called uptwisting. Charlie Harrison, manager of the silk department and Harold Rhead are pictured here

Above: The knitting department. George Robinson, Benjamin Hill's son-in-law, is one of the men on this photograph

Below: The silk balling room at William Hills. The two men are Arthur Tomkinson and Mr Grindrod. Silk bobbins with intricate patterns were hand balled by these men. This thread was used by tailors in Saville Row for the buttonholes on bespoke suits

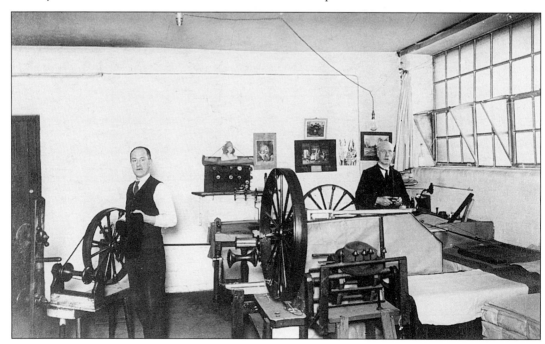

Wardle and Davenport's 'Big Mill' on Mill Street can be clearly seen in this photograph together with the buildings which comprised the Wardle and Davenport complex stretching from Mill Street to Belle Vue. Closer examination of this scene will reveal Goodwin and Tatton's Mill at the top of West Street and Waterloo Mill and the factory opposite once occupied by 'Spun Silk' and now 'Slimma', plus several other factories. Copyright: Aerofilms

Above: An excellent view of Wardle and Davenport's Belle Vue Mills. The company began as a partnership between Henry Wardle from the Britannia Inn and George Davenport, a silk throwster. This leading textile company began with a capital of just £300 and premises in West Street. In 1872 they took over half of a floor in Big Mill which they shared with William Broster and Frederick Hammersley. Wardle and Davenport's eventually purchased Big Mill and another mill in Belle Vue together with land. Over the years the enormous complex of mills, warehouses and offices was consolidated on a site covering several areas

Below: Big Mill dominated the approach into the town from Macclesfield. This Grade 2 listed building still stands though sadly somewhat dilapidated. Built in 1857 to a Sugden design, it was first occupied by Joseph Broster

Albert Povey, aged 23, arrives for work at Wardle and Davenports during the
1960s. By 1968, over 600 people were employed at Wardle and Davenports
making it one of the largest companies in Leek. The business appeared to be
thriving and jobs for a further 100 girls were announced after diversification in
the late 1960s. However, in reality, heavy losses had accrued throughout the 60s
and the firm went into receivership in 1970. Belle Vue Mills were demolished and
a lingerie factory built on the site

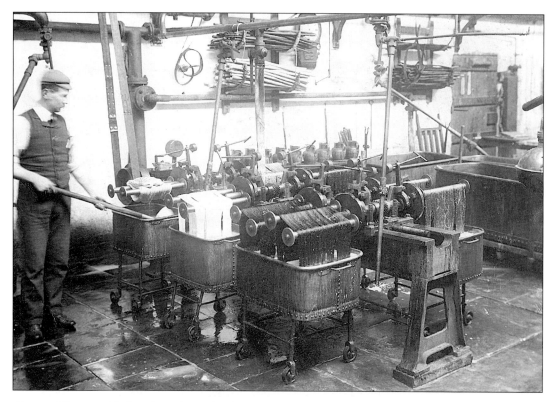

Above: We are told that this photograph was taken in Wardle and Davenports. The authors, who are not experts on the textile industry, believe that the machinery is part of the dyeing process, but we could be wrong!

Right: Clattering machinery crowded into confined spaces. This is the silk braiding department

Left: The Hose Room in June 1953 decorated for the coronation. The large crown hanging from the ceiling was made by Freda Nettel. The ladies pictured are seamers and they include: Gertie Furby, Mary Ogden, Margaret Gethern, Edith Bond, Nellie Pepper, Molly Luton, Edna Biddulph, Irene Nixon, Muriel Pakeman. Edith Frost, Edith Lacey, Jenny Mellor, Phyllis Nettell, Marjorie Bowcock, Audrey Goodfellow, Vera Goldstraw, Nancy Hiscock, Ivy Woolley, Hazel Done and Nancy Lowe. Surrounded by these lovely ladies are Peter Hulme, Tom Stubb (mechanic) and Charles Briand who was in charge. Seams were put into the stockings in this room before they were sent down to the dyehouse. The white stockings can be seen piled in the foreground

Below: The same room now transformed into the scarf and hat room. Mrs Adshead was in charge of this room. Mrs Williams, Nancy Hambleton, Muriel Pakeman and Kathleen Beak can also be seen. Scarves are being overlocked to the right and examined on the left. Besides scarves Wardle and Davenport also made knitted jumpers, coats, frocks, costumes and lingerie

Above: More Coronation festivities in 1953, believed to be Wardles

Below: A group of men who worked in the Hose department at Wardle and Davenports. They knitted the stockings on huge, long knitting machines. Wardles introduced art silk hosiery in the early 1900s and went on to make the famous 'Three Knots' hosiery.

This photograph is thought to have been taken in the 1950s. Included in this photograph are Ken Hambleton, Fred Critchlow, Maurice Bailey, Mr Barnett, Charlie Pointon, Norman Taylor, Charlie Hambleton, Tom Basnett, Vic Edge, Jack Sherratt, Dickie Perkin, Albert Reeves

An advertisement from 1965 showing the range of products made by Wardle and Davenports. Their famous Per-Lusta thread was always used by Howards (featured in this book) to make their high class housecoats

The Big Mill and a towering chimney are all that remain of the Wardle and Davenport's site after demolition in the 1970s. In its heyday the site covered 16 acres and employed 3,000 people

Above: A final check before boxing-up

Below: The machine room

Above: A fascinating view of the factory and surrounding streets

Below: This scene shows well the belt-drive from the steam engine to drive the machinery

Above: All these people appear to be checking garments

Below: In the dyehouse showing skeins of material ready for dyeing

In the early 1880s spun silk was first introduced in Leek by William Watson & Co. Spun silk is thread made from silk waste. The Leek Spun Silk Spinning and Manufacturing Company were operating in London Mills by 1892 before moving to Gordon Mills in James Street (see p.149)

Above: London Mills, London Street

Above: This early photograph is taken at the rear of Watson's mill. Most of the women are wearing white aprons and all of them have their hair up, whether because it was fashionable to do so or to prevent accidents with moving machinery is a moot point. The lady in the second row wearing a scarf is Mrs Harriet Crombie. The men with their hands resting on womens shoulders are married to that particular lady. Such familiarity would not be encouraged between unmarried couples!

Below: Horace White is the only man amongst a group of industrious ladies at Watsons

Above: Watson's dyehouse circa 1930. These men dipped the skeins of silk into the dye baths a requisite number of times in order to obtain the correct shade. If the men began to chat they sometimes forgot the count and the colour would be wrong! George Grindey, a binding weaver, is one of the men pictured here. He was helping out in the dye house

Below: The Sorting room for outwork, after Watsons became a Job White subsidiary

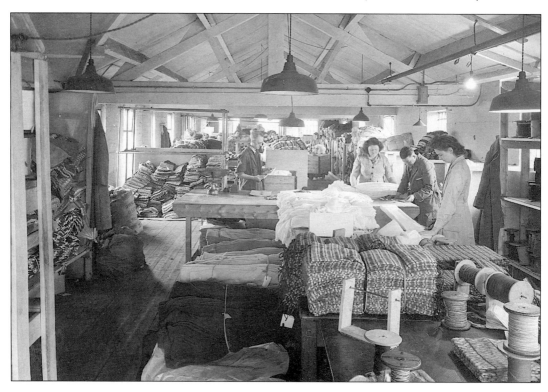

Above: The scarves department, putting on the fringing

Below: The stock room. These two views are also after the purchase by Job Whites

Above: In 1937 nearly all the factories in Leek took on a festive appearance to celebrate the Coronation. Bedecked with streamers, flags, bunting and balloons these cheerful ladies in Old Bank Mill celebrate in style. The two girls in the centre front of this photograph are Nellie Belfield and Gladys Lee

Previous page: The range of threads supplied by Whittles's can be seen here in this display at the Nicholson Institute. The high class silk threads and button hole twists manufactured by the firm were featured in an exhibition held in Leek in the 1940s.

Left: When Wellington Mills was built in 1853 it was surrounded by fields. Even by 1878 it was not crowded by rows of terraced houses which surround it today. Thomas Whittles has always been a family concern and operated in Wellington Mills for many years. Whittle's made silk sewing thread and was the only firm still engaged in the silk industry in Leek by the 1970s. When Thomas Whittle's closed in 1994 it marked the end of the silk industry in Leek. The property has now been converted to residential accommodation

Below: An artist's drawing of Wellington silk mills from the back of a visiting card

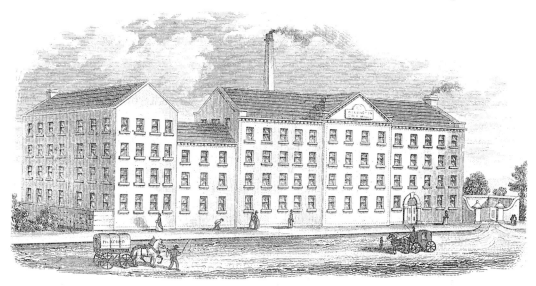

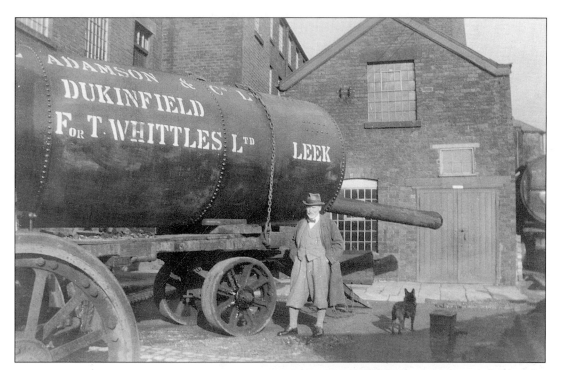

Above: Henry Edward Whittles
stands by his new boiler which he
purchased for the dye house in the
late 1920s. The boiler was conveyed
to the mill on a traction engine from
Daniel Adamson's works in
Dukinfield, Lancashire

Right: The front end of a Cornish
boiler at Whittles photographed in
April 1990

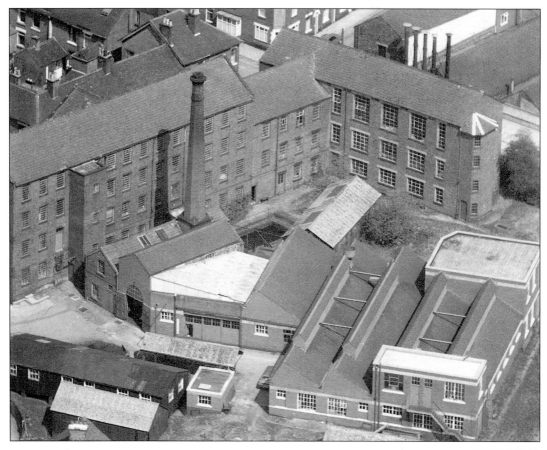

Above: A birds eye view in June 1982 of the site of
Wellington Mills. The mill built in 1853 is on the left at
right angles to an older mill. This older mill was altered so
that a new façade can be seen, however the roof and the
ends of the building were retained. In the mid foreground
are the boiler houses (to the left) and the dye houses (to
the right). The boiler house once held a steam beam
engine which was later replaced by a tandem cylinder
engine. This drove the machinery in the 1853 mill.

The long wooden shed in the left foreground was once
an army hut on Cannock Chase during World War 1; it
was used as a garage for Whittles's cars.

The steam engine from this works may be seen in the
entrance to the Llywernog Silver Lead Mine attraction,
Ponterwyd, north-west of Devils Bridge, mid Wales

Right: This advertisement from 1953 reveals the variety of
threads supplied by Whittles. Thomas Whittles continued
to make high quality button hole thread used by Saville
Row tailors until the firm closed. The 100 years quoted in
this advertisement refers to the 1853 date of Wellington
Mill, in fact it was Messrs Bentley and Whittles who
occupied this mill in the early years

Above: The Counting House

Below: A silk throwing mill – after the spinning process, the silk was thrown – 2 ends for sewing thread and 3 ends for buttonhole twist

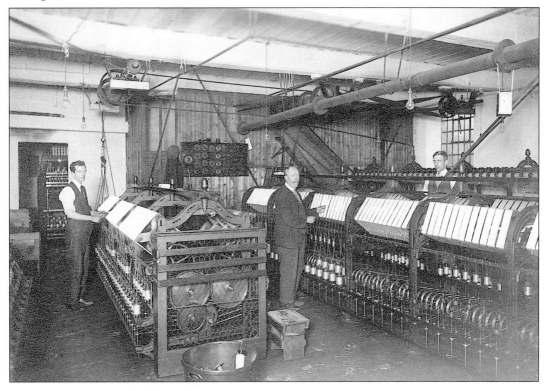

Above: Raw silk winding from hank to bobbin. This room was at the top of the 1853 mill

Below: The original dye house. Thomas Geoffrey Whittles, the dye house director, is on the right

Above: A Style 50 Leesona in the copping room. Among those pictured are W Astles and Harold Lindop

Below: A Rice winding frame used for winding silk to bobbins

Above: The warehouse in the dye house. Here the orders were received and sorted into lot numbers

Below: The Warehouse. The silk skeins are hung on the rafters in sizes before being sent to the dye house to fulfill individual orders. The silk came back in parcels before being sent to the winding and spooling department

Above: Spooling Frames. These ladies wound silk onto bobbins in differing quantities according to the requirements of customers. At Whittles the only trade to which girls could be apprenticed was that of spooling

Below: In this photograph are Marjorie Fowler, neé Jones, George Hill, a director, David Knox MP and Edward Hewitt Whittles. Edward Whittles was a director and the last chairman of the company. He is the great great grandson of Catherine Whittles from Field House and a decendant of Samuel Bowers Whittles who started the business which became Thomas Whittles Ltd

This silk business is believed to have been established in 1803 by James Goostry. In 1845 it became the company we know today as A J Worthington & Co. Two hundred people were employed by Andrew Jukes Worthington in 1861. By the 1960s the company was manufacturing sewing threads,

silk, rayon, nylon and cotton braids together with cords, trimmings and woven smallwares. Throughout the 1960s Worthingtons regularly advertised for staff in the Leek Post and Times.

ESTABLISHED 1803
in the reign of George III

A. J. Worthington & Co. (Leek) Ltd.

Portland & Queen Mills
LEEK
LONDON   GLASGOW

Manufacturers of Sewing Threads in Silk, Nylon, Cotton, Rayon and other Synthetic fibres for all trades. Braids of every kind and for all purposes. Shoe Laces, Fishing Lines, Cords, Girdles, Fancy Trimmings and Fringes for the making up and soft furnishing trades, woven bindings and small-wares, Knitted Neckwear.

In June 1967 they required several ring doublers. In 1996 Worthingtons employed 133 staff in Portland Mill where they manufactured textile trimmings and braids for industrial purposes as well as items for fashion and soft furnishings.

The wooden bridge seen in this photograph links Portland Mill on the left and Queen Mill on the right

Left: This advertisement in a Leek Town Guide of 1955 shows the variety of threads, braids and trimmings made at Worthingtons. Note the trademark at the top which is a leek with the words Leek Make. Did the directors of Worthingtons think that the name Leek derived from the vegetable of that name, which it patently does not, or did they choose it as an easily recognisable connection with 'Leek'

Above: In 1978 A J Worthington's employees celebrated 175 years as textile manufacturers at a dinner at the Hotel Rudyard. Here are some of the workers who attended that dinner, they were all presented with a mug to mark the occasion. Several of the people in this photograph are former Watsons employees, A J Worthingtons bought Watsons in 1953

Right: Enjoying their meal at the Hotel Rudyard are Ursula Mellor, Daisy Higinbotham and Nellie Hansell